From the
Mundane
to the
Magnificent

ABOUT THE AUTHOR

The late Vera Stanley Alder was a successful portrait painter who became fascinated by the 'Ancient Wisdom' —the vast body of information dealing with the meaning and purpose of man himself and the constitution and evolution of the whole universe. She made it her task to simplify and summarize this knowledge, in order to present it to others.

This title is one of a series of books by Alder, including.

THE INITIATION OF THE WORLD

THE FINDING OF THE THIRD EYE

THE FIFTH DIMENSION

From the Mundane
to the Magnificent

Memories and Reflections

VERA STANLEY ALDER

London   **Lucis**   New York

First Edition © Author 1979 - (Rider imprint)

2nd Edition © 2017 Lucis Trust

Third Printing 2023

ISBN 978 085330 1493

British Library Reg.

Contents

1	Introduction	7
2	Settling into the Grange	9
3	The Adventure Begins	21
4	The Solar System	37
5	The Army Arrives	52
6	Inside the Atom	61
7	Bin Acquires a Wife	77
8	Hidden Lives	85
9	Beings Within Man	98
10	At the Earth's Core	113
11	The Answer to it All?	129
12	Former Incarnations	138
13	The Colonel Digs	154
14	I Begin My Campaign	163
15	A Glimpse at the Hierarchy	170
16	Gathering in the Harvest	181
17	Raphael's Vision	189
	Bibliography	203

I

Introduction

Have you considered how everything that is said is radiating through space in a medium not yet understood by scientists, although increasingly used?

Perhaps, in a finer stratum of this medium, everything that ever has been said is also still radiating! Through the existence of telepathy, we realize that everything, including thought, also radiates, and can be picked up by those in resonance with it – so that similar ideas, or inventions, or plans are brought forth around the world. This is more prevalent today than ever before, and amongst more people.

This same phenomenon could also occur with everything *seen*. This would seem to be proved by clairvoyants, and also psychometrists who can recall scenes from the past when touching objects which received past radiations. According to the Ageless Wisdom and modern theosophies, humanity is only at the half-way stage of its potential development. A fundamental extension of its five senses lies ahead, as well as the emergence of yet further senses. These have all been hinted at, for instance, as the gifts of the Holy Ghost.

Examples of such super-development have been demonstrated by certain saints and sages ahead of their times. Many cases of rudimentary sense-extension are amongst us today in such numbers that they have engendered the expression: Extra-Sensory Perception (ESP). So far, however, most cases of sense-extension, such as clairvoyance, clairaudience, psychometry, or healing, are *involuntary*. Only in very advanced exceptions do they become partly *voluntary*.

Voluntary extended capacities lie far ahead of humanity. They will bring a vastly enlarged and varied experience that scarcely could be borne by even an advanced person of today. Nevertheless, in order to possess a necessary sense of life orientation, we must look forward to such developments and prepare for them – if indeed humanity is on the way to maturity.

Science is teaching us, through the medium of X-ray, wireless and television, that we can no longer deny the possibility of our own potentials in the worlds of radiation. Could we – and will we – learn to plug our minds in to various wavelengths, some of which come from outside our solar system? Why not? Such achievement would necessitate special training which is not yet available – *but if it were?*

This book contains a description of such an experience. How much of it is true or possible, or whether it is a vision due to wishful thinking, must be left to the reader to decide. The background of these experiences – an Essex village in wartime – is exactly true, although the personalities touched upon are not authentic – only typical, including, perhaps, Raphael himself.

The existence of spiritual guides, or 'gurus', is becoming of world-wide interest, catered for in countless groups of varied quality – to the degree that the seeker finds his powers of discrimination tried to their utmost. Only through the resonance of his own integrity can he follow the golden thread of Truth to its ultimate fulfilment – and this is a hard but glorious pilgrimage.

2

Settling into the Grange

After my first book was published I really did not know what to expect, because the whole situation was quite new to me. When letters from readers began to arrive, I could hardly believe in the enthusiasm which they expressed. I had written about things which I deeply felt to be true, but with which I had only recently become acquainted. I agreed fully with the study that I had made of the Ageless Wisdom in its modern form; but I realized that my knowledge was only second-hand, and that I needed my imagination to visualize the reality of that which I had accepted as the Truth. This gave me a very restless feeling. I recognized that the intellectual approach may be sounder than the emotional one, because the emotions could carry you further from the truth than could logical theorizing.

By the time I found myself thoroughly settled into country life, and 'far from the madding crowd' of London, I knew that for the first time in my life I had leisure to do much thinking and self-training, in accordance with what I had learned, as well as exploring the potential of my own 'psychic' capacities. I deeply felt the need for a further step forward, in order to turn teaching and imagination into a real experience of all I had learned. This need became more intense every day. I remembered the saying: 'When the pupil is ready the Master will appear'. I recalled the instances I had read of the appearance of a 'guru' when the aspiring neophyte was desperate for more progress.

However, these were tales of the past and tales of the East. Could I possibly hope for such an experience in the prosaic English countryside? After all, why not? The Truth, and the teaching, were surely not confined to one part of the planet! As this possibility took root in my mind it became more and more intense, more and more urgent, until the idea was almost ever-present, thus making me increasingly desperate. How could I possibly start to achieve a first-hand understanding of what I had learnt? How could I conjure up a teacher, even if I deserved one? The days passed with an ever-increasing obsession and longing for the achievement of first-hand knowledge.

One day, at last, something happened. I will tell you exactly what occurred: it is for you to judge whether it was my imagination, brought on by wishful thinking, or to what extent these were actual events. Anyway, I will describe it as if it did really happen, which will be the simplest thing to do. Naturally, I continued with my outer life, my life of gardening and of identifying with the progress of the war. Outwardly, I was working on the land, a land-girl on our own land, and what was more, all alone on our own land, just as my cousin Marion was all alone in our big house. Therefore, when strange things began to happen to me I was not tempted to tell anyone about them, because there was no one to tell except Marion, and I felt that she would have been worried about me if I had told her. So in the end I was leading a sort of double life, as you will see.

The war had scattered my family in all directions, and that is why by 1940 Marion and I were alone on the family property. Our Grange, not moated, had once been a monastery, whose industrious inhabitants had made beer and wine, and planted beautiful walnut trees. There were five wells within the walls of the house and the enormous barn. The latter contained a huge vat which would have made a good swimming pool. From the grounds one heard nothing of the quiet little village in which it was set, the village of Sybil Hedingham, surrounded, as it was, by rolling open country.

Peaceful it had always been, but by 1940 it had become obvious that we were under the direct air-route which the Germans took to bomb London, and below which many of our marching regiments passed regularly on their way to the channel ports. Therefore, our life was gradually becoming a strange mixture of rustic peace and violent danger.

My first book, *The Finding of the Third Eye*, had been published in 1938. I was still dazed and unbelieving that I had really written a book. The encouraging letters that were reaching me, especially from overseas, made me feel more unreal than ever. The fact that I had been uprooted from my portrait-painter's studio in London, and planted down in a strange countryside and told by my family to take charge of our newly-acquired estate, as my war job, made life still more unreal. The fact that I knew exactly nothing about gardening, or vegetable growing, having always been a town-dweller, seemed to worry nobody. It was apparently up to me to overcome that slight disadvantage.

I was blessed with a rather fascinating family, about whom much could be written. But as this book is neither about my family nor even about myself – but is all about my extraordinary experiences, I will not bring my family into it – and those people whom I do describe will be, as I said, typical rather than authentic. So my story starts from the time when the last of my family had left en route for a post in the USA leaving me in charge of the four-acre estate, whilst our kind elderly cousin, whom I will call 'Marion', was to take charge of the large Grange itself.

Marion was a rather orthodox person, and probably

considered me as eccentric, as I am afraid my family did, because of my new book and my tendency to become a 'cranky vegetarian'. However, we did see eye to eye very happily in our love of Bin, the family mascot, who was, of course, the most important member of our household. Much elevated from human status, he was a snow-white hare, born in Tibet, and raised in Peking.

Both Bin and Marion were looking very wistful after the last wave of good-bye to the departing family. I tried to cheer her up. 'I'll grow you lovely salads and gorgeous strawberries,' I promised, 'but how on earth do I begin? I must buy a gardening book at once!'

It was lucky that I had a studious nature. With the usual Scorpio enthusiasm I was soon deep in my new gardening books. I discovered that the whole process was far more involved and tricky than I had imagined. One might almost say that it was quite a science. You did everything that you were supposed to do, and then for some subtle reason things would go wrong. There would be this kind of blight, or that sort of mould. The soil would be too light, or too heavy, or too acid. In fact I had already heard men talking deeply and importantly on the subject over the radio.

I found myself looking at the soil with new eyes. I realized that until then I had hardly been aware of it, only thinking of it as a dark substance of a colour I did not like. It had a habit of getting into the wrong places. It looked better covered up with juicy green grass or flowers. Now, suddenly, it took on a new aspect. It was to be an enemy or a friend whom I had to master. Anyway, I would have to start by digging it. If we were to have salads and vegetables throughout the winter, of which I was determined, there was not a moment to lose, and I must plan the whole programme at once.

I glanced around the large walled garden where I was sitting. Then I stood up and fetched a heavy spade. With a tremendous thrust I drove it against the silent dark

Bin *the Tibetan Hare, Tibet's symbol of wisdom*

soil. My wrists received a violent wrench, and the soil had apparently taken no notice of my action whatever. Again and again I tried. My wrists were thin, my muscles, it seemed, were non-existent. Doggedly, I went in search of some easier tools. Sure enough, I found a medium-sized fork that I could wield with more effect. In a moment I had heaved up my first clod of soil, and turned it over on to its side with a thump. Oh, the triumph of it! I could really dig!

An hour afterwards, tousled, boiling hot and very masterful, I had produced what looked like a small bomb crater. I looked proudly at Higgs, the old gardener, as he came lumbering up the path.

'Whatever you a doin' of, Miss?' he queried anxiously.

'Doing, Mr. Higgs? Why, I'm getting this ground ready for sowing for the autumn and winter salads. I'm digging it first.'

'Diggin', did you say? *Diggin'?* But where's your top spit?'

I was on the verge of telling him that I didn't spit when I was digging, but I stopped myself in time.

'Spit?' I queried, trying to give him a lead.

The old man seized the neglected spade, spat on his hands (now I understood!), drove the spade deep, deep into the ground, brought it up again with a neat square of earth balanced upon it, which he laid carefully in a selected spot. After repeating this a score of times he pointed out to me that he had produced a tidy little trench with a tidy little regiment of clods above it.

'There's yer first spit,' he remarked quietly, 'and down below it is yer second spit – and yer mustn't mix them, see? Well, goodday Miss, I'll be off home now.'

Higgs was our last remaining gardener. All the younger ones had already been enlisted, leaving him alone to tackle our four acres on his two mornings a week – all that could be spared from neighbouring work. No-one had dared to tell him that I was scheduled to manage the garden. One knew that gardeners could be rather touchy.

'How on earth do I arrange not to mix them?' I thought, gazing down on the arrangements of soil beneath me. 'I do hope I can find out from my *Gardeners' Guide*. And I shall have to manage without spitting – I simply couldn't!'

Reluctantly I began to put my tools away. Curiously enough I seemed to want to go on digging, or trying to – on, and on, and on! In fact, I had been enjoying myself. There seemed to be a sort of fascination about it. Somehow, one could not stop. Even if it was tea-time, or getting dark one wanted to go on and on – not only with the digging but with any other kind of job there was to do. This fascination seemed steadily to grow, causing me to work harder and harder every day. The feeling that I was creating something, producing growing creatures, had proved irresistible.

Autumn deepened into winter, one of the coldest for many years, without driving me indoors. I had rigged myself up in riding breeches, huge warm socks and a pullover. I had coped with snow, ice and wind, finding that the call and urge of the garden could beat my hitherto chronic aversion to the cold. My work done, I would return to the large house, also cold and empty except for Marion's little room.

Marion, with the kettle on, a roaring fire, and her radio going full-blast, with Bin sitting in attendance when it was too cold for him outdoors – that was what I always knew I would find. The kitchen where we ate in company with the huge warm boiler stove, made up the rest of our daily routine. Our drawing-room and dining-room were useless in the winter weather because we could not obtain enough fuel.

Ever since her arrival, Marion had sought company and consolation in her radio. She followed almost every programme with zest. During this first winter of the war, she seemed almost to live inside the small red box! The resounding voice of Churchill used to fill her little room like a presence, whilst she sparkled and nodded as if she were making the speech herself. Her only other pre-occupation was to try and feed me and Bin to the best of her ability in spite of the growing difficulties of rationing. Our greatest thrill was the arrival of the postman with letters from America from my family, telling as much as would pass the censor.

One of my tasks was to do the local shopping. In that way I had begun to know a few neighbours and to hear the local gossip. It always seemed to be about illnesses! In that charming little village with the fresh sweet air sweeping through it, far from traffic fumes and smoking factories, almost everyone was suffering from some com-plaint. There were many slowly dying from cancer, tuberculosis, heart failure and a variety of other diseases. As for the animals, either it was foot-and-mouth disease, fowl pest, or many worse things. Even the trees and crops seemed doomed to endless forms of blight and pest.

I was becoming very puzzled. I had always thought of the country as a healthy place. In fact, it *felt* healthy. The sun almost embraced one, and sometimes the air fresh-ened one into exhilaration. One could have been happy except for the war.

I mentioned that the Grange was exactly underneath the route that the German bombers took, to and from London. Any bombs that were left over were dropped on the way back on anything that looked like an airfield or a factory. Marion, Bin and I used the pantry as our air-raid shelter because it had the thickest walls. We would tuck ourselves in, wireless and all, trying not to get too chilled, grateful when we could creep back to our warm beds once more.

So, eventually, the winter had passed, and the days had begun to lengthen. I waited eagerly for the time when I could begin my planting and sowing. By then, I was feeling like an experienced and full-fledged gardener. Marion had arranged to have some hens sent to me, in the hope that we could have our own eggs. This meant much extra work, but oh the pride of collecting those eggs – although it did seem unkind to take them away.

In fact, the result of my first six months on the land was not making me feel very happy. I was so full of questions that no-one could answer for me. Why was there this horrible war? Why, even without war, was there so much poverty, so much illness, so much ineptitude, such slow, automatic thinking, such preoccupation with tiny mundane ways? Surely there were remedies, solutions, to these urgent troubles? Why did no-one want to think about it? To eat, to sleep, to grow vegetables and meats, to nurse a vast concourse of invalids, and to discuss them in pubs! – was this all there was to life in the country?

History had taught me about a long procession of geniuses, artists, architects, philosophers, scientists, and wonderful teachers. But what had it all added up to? The Germans, in spite of all their culture, were doing unutterable things to their fellow-beings. The Allies seemed almost obliged to reply in kind. Beautiful landscapes were being churned up into a sea of gory mud. No-one seemed to have any solution, except to go on bravely fighting until one side was tired out.

But there must be a solution to it all. God was certainly real. I had only to look at a flower or an insect or a sunset to be convinced of the existence of a marvellous Creator.

Why then was everything in such a mess? Sometimes I tried to ask Marion such questions.

She would look at me doubtfully.

'Darling, I think you are working too hard in that garden! Why don't you go down to the cinema sometimes? Or, if you feel so – er – depressed, why not go to church a bit more often? That's probably what you need.'

There was, however, no answer for me in church. I blamed myself for that.

'I suppose I'm not really religious' I thought 'but I cannot resolve the things Christ taught with the way people live – and so I only get confused. The most complacent of the church people seem to be the ones who disobey the most commandments.'

I had begun to realize that although I had written a book which purported to explain the answers to all life's problems and the mysteries of the Universe and of the Ageless Wisdom, none of it seemed to be helping *me*, the author, very much! I had come to feel that my acquired knowledge, so enthusiastically declaimed in my book, was in fact *second-hand*. I had accepted and adopted it all with great joy, because it made sense to me, because it gave logical reasons for the conditions and the emergencies of life, and because it held out promises of a glorious future for mankind.

The postulates of reincarnation and of Karma, or cause and effect, had answered so many riddles and had provided a pattern of justice and fair chance for all. That was what I had needed, and judging by my readers' letters it was what they needed also. But was it in the end, really enough? In spite of the Ageless Wisdom, in spite of all the beautiful teachings at man's disposal throughout history, wars still continued, and the most unspeakable and unthinkable horrors were perpetrated by those very human beings who were supposed to have 'God within them'.

I could understand the necessity for a certain amount of 'evil', in order to learn by the Law of Contrasts. But I could not face up to the steadily increasing extremes of wickedness, the capacity for wholesale destruction, endless cruelties to men and animals – the exploitation of Mother Earth and of people's own bodies. I could not see why people, who could express so much of genius, of beauty and of goodness, could be so blind to the other side of the picture.

Where was the real root of this problem? How could this situation be changed? There was evidently still a great deal which one did not know, a section of knowledge still hidden, but which might provide the ultimate clue. I racked my brains in vain to think what it could be.

Gradually, this questioning, tormented state of mind increased in me until one day I found that I could not even enjoy my gardening any more – just when I had expected to be most thrilled with it. For the month of February was nearly over. The first shoots were up everywhere, and it was time for me to get down to my sowing and planting in earnest.

As I straightened my back and looked down at my beautifully dug salad beds with their rows of coloured thread, and little gleaming pegs, all so expert and orderly, I did not feel the usual pride. I stood there with a sensation of loneliness, futility and desperation.

What was I doing it all for – just the same as everyone else, even if a little better, perhaps? Why, – when there was no result except war, illness, widespread poverty, even stupidity – although in some ways people knew so much, and had achieved so many marvels?

What was the sense of it – what was the use of it all? There must be some answer! There had to be! I wanted to *know!* I *must* know much more about life than I did. There must be things to know which I had not even dreamt of as yet. I almost stamped upon the ground!

Sensing that all was not well with his friend, Bin left his work of digging and chewing, and lolloped up to me, licking my shoes anxiously.

I picked him up and held him closely. He was my only companion most of the day. What a pity that he could not talk. Perhaps he knew more than anyone else? Anyway, he knew how to keep himself healthy, happy and serene. What was his secret?

Animals always seem to know what to do.

Why was humanity so muddled?

Dejectedly, I turned away from my beloved salad beds, and, settling Bin comfortably across my shoulder, I left the walled garden and wandered slowly back towards the Grange.

3

The Adventure Begins

My mood of unrest continued throughout the evening. Even a quite dramatic radio play failed to distract me. At last I slipped away, almost unnoticed by the enthralled Marion, and by Bin equally engrossed in performing his evening toilet.

With a sigh, I entered my own quiet room. It was flooded in silver moonlight. In fact the moon was full, and shining straight on to my little divan. Quickly I slipped out of my garden clothes and flung myself upon it. My feeling of desperation was still engulfing me. In the whole of Essex there seemed to be no-one with whom I could speak, no-one who could give me any answers, or who was interested even in trying to do so.

The room was warm, because the fire still glowed and crackled redly but the light from the moon was cold, withdrawn, silent, mysterious. Why was there such a difference between these two lights? Were they both made of the same thing? Surely they had different powers, influences?

'Oh I'm so *tired* of knowing nothing – nothing *real*, nothing helpful. I need *personal* knowledge – not second-hand! That's what is the matter with me. I feel starved, full up with theory, but devoid of fact.'

The depths of my despairing desire were so overwhelming that I started to sob. Within a few moments I was weeping more wildly than I had ever done in my life. This longing of mine was stronger than anything I had known before. It even amounted to a prayer. 'Oh God!' I whispered chokingly, 'please help me – You know what I want!'

I had not prayed like that for years. Astonished at myself, I opened my eyes and sat up.

Standing in the room, silhouetted against the moonlight, was a tall, silent figure.

I caught my breath. Curiously enough, I did not feel frightened. The man, for it was a man, spoke to me at once.

'So you want to *know*, Verity?'

The voice was very quiet, gentle but vibrant.

'Yes . . . yes!' I answered with my last sob, gazing up at the stranger with growing astonishment. How did he know my name – my family's pet name for me, because I was always after the truth? I saw that he was bearded, with deep glittering eyes. He seemed to be wearing some sort of long coat. He looked very calm.

'What is it, exactly, that you want to know?' he repeated.

I considered carefully. I felt that it might be an important question.

'Well, I want to know those things which most intelligent people do not yet know.'

'Which things?' came again the steady voice.

'The world is in a mess – isn't it?' I burst out eagerly. 'That must be because of things which people do not know – radical things, which would make them act differently!'

I felt that my explanation was very bald and inadequate.

'Why do you want to know such things?' The tone was stern.

'In order to help them, of course!' I said immediately.

'Of *course*?' echoed the stranger, as if in doubt.

'Why else should I?' I wondered in answer.

'Some people want knowledge as a personal possession!'
he replied.

'Without using it to help? That would be wrong!' and
I really felt scornful about that.

The bearded man kept silent for a moment. Then he
seemed to relax, to make up his mind about something.

'Verity!' he began, 'I see that you have the right motive
– and that is everything in life. You want knowledge in
order that you may help people by spreading it – as you
have already begun to do, is that so?'

'That makes me sound like a propagandist!'

'Or a teacher? Teachers are born, you know, not made.
You, my dear friend, are suffering from what is known as
the "Divine Discontent". That is a good illness. Perhaps
I can grant your wish. What is it that you want to know?'

Once again, an important question, I felt. This time I
did not hestitate.

'The Truth – I want to *see* the Truth for myself, instead
of relying on so many teachings, some of which seem
contradictory, and different in different cultures. I want
to know what we can do to get rid of all the evil and
misery in the world. I want to know what this planet
really is. I want to know the Truth about disease – about
sin – about . . . .'

'So! You are certainly going to overwork me if I teach
you all that!' interrupted the stranger, almost smiling.
'You are asking for a great privilege. Do you not realize
that Truth is dangerous? Or that, if I told you the whole
Truth you are not ready or able to grasp it? You have
not yet even the brain cells which could accept Truth –
most people have not! I will therefore, have to *translate*
Truth, set it down to the stage where you will begin to
understand it. I cannot teach you the ultimate Truth yet,
but only the next steps towards it, for *you!* Do you understand?'

'I think so. But how are you going to *translate* it?' I
asked, puzzled.

'I am going to teach you through your eyes – visually. I can use my will to alter the focus of your eyes so that you gradually see more of what there is to see. You will have to trust me to explain to you little by little whilst your mind and brain are *growing*. For they will have to grow quite new cells in order to manage unaccustomed ways of thinking. So you must be patient. And please remember that all that I show you will be strictly provable from the so-called scientific angle. Now we will begin!'

My heart was already beating fast with excitement. At last the longed-for moment was arriving.

'I am dying with suspense!' I pleaded.

The bearded man smiled with great sympathy.

'Then tell me first of all,' he said quietly, 'are you able to distinguish between yourself – and your body?'

'Certainly! the real Me is surely a spirit – an invisible being – imprisoned tightly within this human frame?'

'Not quite so tightly as you imagine. Now I will show you something. Are you afraid to leave your body?'

I drew myself together in instinctive alarm. This was unexpected. Then I remembered the issue at stake.

'No! no! Not if you think it necessary,' I replied, wondering just what he meant.

'Excellent!' he commented, satisfied. 'Now will you remember that if you should be afraid you can always call on me. My name is Raphael.'

'Raphael!' I repeated, liking the name. 'But you will stay near me won't you?'

'I will be with you all the time. Actually you will be perfectly safe. Now, relax yourself and breathe more and more slowly and steadily. We can only do this experiment when you are quite, quite calm.'

I was determined to help him as much as possible. I lay back against the cushions and closed my eyes. My heart was still thundering in my ears. That evidently would not do. I forced myself to breathe deeply and quietly, and ever more slowly. I even felt that Raphael was helping me in some way. In fact I began to have a faint memory as of something familiar in this situation. Gradually it seemed that my breathing was establishing a kind of rhythm in my body. I became aware of peculiar feelings within myself: something like the rotating of wheels. It seemed as if there were several wheels whirling within me as if the inside of my body was like a watch. Even as I was thinking about this, the movements changed. It seemed as if the wheels suddenly reversed and were going round the other way. There came a peculiar revulsion of feeling all through me. For a moment I felt terrible, much worse than a person feels who is going to faint. But the wheels were speeding up tremendously! Soon it seemed as if I was being whirled around too. I gasped for breath and tried not to scream. Then I opened my eyes and found myself clinging to the arm of the bearded man.

'Oh, I'm so sorry!' I cried. 'I really didn't mean to move!' Raphael held my hands firmly within his.

'Have you moved or haven't you?' he asked mysteriously, nodding his head towards my divan.

I looked round swiftly. There I was, lying outstretched, seemingly asleep! For an instant I gazed fascinated. It was a view of myself that I had never seen, with eyes closed and lashes sweeping downwards on my pale cheeks. I looked at Raphael to see if he were satisfied. His smile reassured me. Then I looked down at myself standing by his side. I had a shock. I could see nothing – nothing at all!

'But where am I?' I stammered, feeling really afraid. 'Which is me? Am I dead?'

'Steady! Steady,' admonished Raphael gripping my hands tightly, 'or you will spoil the experiment! Of course you – your body – is not dead. If you watch you can see it breathing. Of course the real you is standing by me. *You* have merely slipped out of your physical body!'

I looked anxiously at Raphael. He stood beside me, solid as a rock, his rough sleeve crinkled where my invisible hand was clutching it.

'Now I will confess to you,' he said, chuckling gently, 'that I am playing a little trick upon you. You are not seeing things as they really are! But this is the only way in which I can gradually make certain facts clear to you. I have helped you to leave your physical body, *but* I have caused you to retain only your physical eyesight for the moment. So you are still using those optic nerves which react only through physical or solid matter. Think of X-ray! It sees more than you do. But it is still only a comparatively clumsy or tentative instrument. Later, they will be able to adjust this to many finer vibrational rates, or wave-lengths. But your eyes are marvellous instruments, although largely unused as yet. Now watch! I will bring your finer optical senses into play and you shall see a more subtle grade of physical matter!'

So saying, he passed his hands gently over my head. I continued to stare in fascination at the divan and the prone figure of myself – or my body – upon it. There I was, lying apparently asleep, and seemingly quite intact, and unaware of what was happening. At this point I realized that, indeed, something *was* happening – to my eyes!

The solid form of myself upon the divan seemed to be darkening, to be losing its fleshlike colour, and to be growing less distinct. I began to feel somewhat queer and faint. Was there, then, nothing of me that was solid anywhere? I strained my sight anxiously, and as I gazed I began to be aware of a new quality about that body. I saw a faint phosphorescent glow emanating from it.

I watched patiently, waiting until my senses should become accustomed to this new quality of eyesight, just as one waits to be able to distinguish things in a dark room.

Soon I could see that there really was a beautiful delicate blue light which spread through all the flesh, giving it a hollow, transparent look.

Suddenly, I drew back with a shudder. I had discovered that I was looking right *through* my recumbent form. I could see the bones, and vague and shadowy, the organs, veins and sinews. I could watch my ribs swelling and sinking gently through my breathing. I struggled between a feeling of nausea and of intense, fascinated interest.

'Remember, we are still dealing with purely normal and physical things,' announced my companion rather sternly, as if to curb my amazement. 'As I told you, the X-ray can see as you see now! I have merely stimulated that same ray which is of course a part of your own composition, too. We can all have X-ray sight when suitably developed. A few already have it. You call them "clairvoyants." But there are very many degrees and stages. Now watch whilst I strengthen your sight still further.'

I watched obediently. But to my disappointment the body upon the bed became ever fainter and more ethereal-looking to my eyes. At the same time, the blue light which permeated it grew stronger. It was rather beautiful. It extended quite evenly for about an inch outside the skin. It seemed to shimmer softly with quivering life. 'Surely now I am looking at the etheric double?' I whispered.

'It is Life!' was the the reply. 'Life as it flows through living ether. Go nearer and study it.'

I approached and strained my sight upon this strange phenomenon. Gradually I perceived that this enveloping blue light took on to perfection the form it permeated. It was actually a second body, interpenetrating my own physical one. Every bone, every little vein was duplicated. I looked closer. At last I realized that what I saw was not just a phosphorescent glow, as I had at first supposed. It was, indeed, a complete and firmly knit body. It was composed of millions of tiny interlaced threads, fine as the finest spider's web. The whole of the fleshly body, down to the smallest vein, I now saw, was built around this fine webbing. Along each tiny thread raced a flow of blue light, transforming it into a living neon wire.

As I gazed upon this marvellous and beautiful body of living cobweb, the fleshly form through which it ran looked by comparison dark and hollow.

'Is this really me?' I asked in wonderment.

'Yes, my friend,' was the reply. 'You are now looking at your *real* physical body, that which feeds and forms and builds what we call the solid one. It is named, as you quoted, the "body of ether" or the "etheric body." It forms a link between the inner chemical matter which composes your body as you know it, and the electrical forces of life which can reach it only through the medium of the ether.'

I continued to gaze unbelievingly.

'Of course I have read about the etheric body – but do you say that everyone is like this?' I asked at last.

'Every person, every animal, every plant – everything in fact which depends for its growth upon what we may describe as the "electrical energies" which can only travel through the medium of the ether. All these living things must each have their own "double" or organized ether body, to act as a conductor.'

I turned my eyes quickly to the window to look at the familiar trees outside. Sure enough I now saw them outlined and permeated by the same beautiful fine blue webbing. I had always thought of a tree as a lovely creation, but seen thus it was ten times more exquisite.

'How wonderful it all looks,' I murmured, 'but somehow those trees look more complete than I do . . ' and I turned my eyes once more to the figure upon the divan, noticing little patches and spaces that interrupted the fine webbing here and there.

'You are observant, Verity,' declared Raphael with apparent satisfaction. 'The blemishes which you see are temporary only – they are due to your distressed condition. It is thus that a clairvoyant can diagnose internal ills in any part of the body. Of course it is not easy, because the physical senses are unaccustomed to looking right through an object.'

I was enthralled with my new eyesight. I felt as if I could continue to study the form upon the divan for ever.

'Tell me, please, Raphael, are there others who can come out of their bodies as I have done?'

The bearded man smiled gently.

'All human beings are capable of it after a little training,' he replied. 'But in this age most people are concerning themselves entirely with the mastery of the outer visible world. They are neglecting and forgetting their own powers at this period of history. Nevertheless, unknown to themselves, they each live duplicate lives. Most people leave their bodies and travel in various ways at night.'

'Then I suppose that's what's called "having a dream",' I pondered. 'Of course I *have* written about it!'

'Are you ready, my friend,' enquired my companion at last, 'to learn more about that Self which is standing here beside me – containing the real You?' and he smiled into my eyes.

'*You* can evidently see me!' I said jealously as I made a vain effort to discover any trace of myself in the empty space beneath my eyes.

'I do see you perfectly,' was the response. 'Don't look so anxious! You will know more in a moment. Now, follow my argument carefully. The real You is swayed by emotions and feelings, is it not, quite often?'

'Very often!' I agreed emphatically.

'Quite so. The real You can either be ruled by violent feelings or can rise superior to them, can it not?'

'Oh, yes – one is sometimes mastered by one's emotions in spite of the combined strength of one's will-power, common sense and actual wishing!'

'I am glad you have observed as much. Therefore the feelings are separate forces to the mind or to the will?'

'Why, yes – of course they must be! And that is what I have read – and written, anyway,' said I, somewhat doubtfully.

'Without the emotions we should have no driving force, no incentive, no attractions, no love! The emotions compose the impetus which drives us into every action.' He turned to me suddenly. 'What are they made of?'

'Made of?' I echoed, somewhat stupified.

'Yes! Think! That violent rush of emotion which almost chokes your body and quite paralyses your mind! It must belong to a different world – made of what?'

'Er – electricity?' I hazarded.

'Consider again, my friend. Electricity obeys certain regular laws. Emotions are lawless and irregular. Actually, there is a whole world of emotion-stuff, just as there is a world of ethers, and it also interpenetrates the living entity whom it drives into action. Each creature must therefore have an organized body of this emotion-stuff also, so that he can take part in the emotional world (the astral world as it is called). Would you like to see it? Shall I stimulate your astral sight, which is really an extension of your physical sight?'

'Yes,' I whispered, trying to remember all I knew about the astral plane.

'Very well! But as astral atoms are much finer than physical and etheric atoms you cannot see both physically and astrally at the same time. Now watch!'

He made a slow movement with his hand before my face, or the place where my face should have been.

I glared anxiously at the body upon the divan outlined in its beautiful phosphorescent webbing. As I watched, the flesh and bones gradually faded from my vision. So did the solid wooden structure of the divan. Yet I could still see them, somehow!

I blinked and stared. I realized that indeed they were still visible, but they seemed to be formed of a kind of vibrating thick grey smoke. I turned to my companion.

I saw with a shock that he also was formed of this thick smoke-like substance. I looked down at the place where my own limbs should be. I discovered with a happy sense of possession that I could certainly see them at last, even if they did look completely strange in their cloud-like form.

A sudden thought struck me.

'Why,' I cried, 'we look just like ghosts!'

A ghostly smile showed above the beard of my companion.

'Exactly!' he agreed. 'A ghost is usually someone who has slipped off his outer physical sheath as we have, either temporarily or permanently, and is seen by accident by those who have not!'

I looked at my companion, my mind working rapidly.

'Yes – but,' I objected at last, 'there is my body upon the divan! But where is yours?'

Raphael looked away from me. 'That question, my friend, I cannot answer yet. It must remain a mystery at present. Now let go of my arm. You are quite safe.'

I complied reluctantly, feeling rather naked and helpless in my tenuous form.

Raphael retired quickly to the far corner of the room. 'Come here!' he commanded.

I hesitated, swaying. How should I control these mysterious limbs of mine?

'Don't be silly!' laughed my new teacher. 'Are you afraid of your own Self? Come here!'

I echoed his laughter and determined to go quickly to him. At that very instant I was by his side.

'How did I get here? I didn't walk!' I asked in surprise.

'Aha! There's something more to think about! You must learn that astral stuff is completely different from physical matter and its reactions. It is finer and more rapid of motion than the ether along which electricity and other forces travel. That means that in your astral body you can travel more quickly than electricity – if you will. Astral stuff is non-physical so it is beyond the laws of gravitation.'

'So that's why I feel as if I'm floating instead of walking – just as I feel in dreams,' I exclaimed.

'Of course! A dream is often a real experience. Now I will strengthen your astral sight a little more. Watch!'

I gazed round the room which seemed like a living picture all in grey. And it was as if dawn broke slowly and mysteriously through everything, from within. It all seemed to light up with a delicate, subtle radiance. This light grew stronger and more definite, until I saw that it was made up of many dancing colours. It was like rays of coloured lights floating very rapidly in various directions, interlacing, mixing, separating, blending, but never still. The whole atmosphere was full of this living, shimmering colour which eddied hither and thither as if blown and twisted by currents of wind. The objects in the room seemed permeated by these colours too. The grey smoky substance was lit up as if each of its particles were part of a wonderful rainbow.

I then looked closely at Raphael. I could see that his body was complete in every detail although formed out of this shimmering fog-like substance. I also noticed that he seemed to be standing within a large filmy globe. This globe stretched out for about half a yard all round him. It puzzled me enormously. It was as if he were standing in the midst of a great soap-bubble. I remembered blowing such beautiful coloured bubbles as a child. I could recollect the joy which I had experienced as I had closely watched the gorgeous filmy colours chasing each other rapidly over their surfaces. Here and now the effect was somewhat the same, except that the colours were not only upon the surface, but were playing in inter-mingling layers all through the bubble.

I moved to one side to alter my view. I noticed that some of the colours moved with me. This was rather muddling. I was not surprised to hear Raphael, who always seemed to read my thoughts, laughing gently. 'You are becoming confused between my aura and your own! Don't forget that you have one too – quite a nice one on the whole, although I do not much like those patches of dark red!'

'Why not?' I asked, squinting intently into the atmosphere surrounding me in an effort to distinguish the eddying colours of my own 'bubble' from the fainter ones surrounding it and the pale brilliance of my companion's radiations.

'Because they indicate a passionate temper,' answered Raphael. 'I should like to see them changed to a purer rose colour. You see, all our emotions are coloured! One can actually be green with envy! Yellow with cowardice, or blue with melancholy! In an unevolved person the colours are dark and turgid, but as one seeks the light of Truth, that light literally irradiates one, and the colours gradually grow brighter and lighter, until they fuse back into one perfect original white light. Then you have the perfect human being, surrounded, not with a coloured aura, but with a halo of light.'

'Just as in the old pictures of the saints!' I exclaimed.

'Exactly! The people who originally painted such pictures simply painted what they saw.'

I peered a little ashamedly at the murky threads of dark colour which I could now discern running through my own aura.

'What's the use of a halo anyway!' I muttered somewhat enviously, trying to locate any dark colours in my companion's beautiful bubble.

Raphael chuckled quite loudly for him.

'You are like an enfant terrible who always asks "why". It is the surest way of arriving at the Truth. But,' and here his voice dropped to a serious note, 'your questions about haloes involve us in a consideration of one of the greatest of mysteries. In order to explain it to you I must take you on a long journey. So tomorrow you must be prepared to go thousands of miles away from your body. How will you like that?'

I looked at him uncertainly, and then towards my own form upon the divan. I was afraid, afraid of the unknown.

'Well . . . I . . . Is it safe? Will I be able to get back here again?' I enquired hesitating.

'That is a natural enough question,' conceded Raphael. 'But look more closely. Perhaps you will discover something . . . .'

I followed his glance and carefully studied the atmosphere between my prone physical body and my 'astral' self. I suddenly saw that there was a thin glowing thread linking the two together. I moved further away. The thread stretched. I pressed nearer to the divan and the thread shortened.

'Well!' I exclaimed, immensely intrigued. 'It's almost like a thread from which the spider hangs. It seems to lengthen and shorten quicker than thought.'

'That is a very good simile!' came Raphael's answer. 'In fact the spider and his web are recognized symbols for some of the most wonderful secrets of the universe. This thin thread which you see is your life-line – the "silver cord" of our Bible. It is linked with your heart and it threads through all your different sub-selves. When it snaps, the body is cast off and you can return to it no more. It can stretch a million miles. But if, whilst you are far away, anything should disturb your sleeping body the message is flashed along this thread and you are snapped back with a rather uncomfortable jerk!'

I shook my head over this, unbelievingly.

'Do you mean to say that all the millions of people on earth have these life-lines and travel all over the place while they sleep? I should think these lines would get hopelessly mixed up and there wouldn't be enough room for them all!'

'My dear friend, you will have to alter your ideas entirely. Things do not need *room* except when in the physical world. You must try to understand the fourth dimension, as you call it. When you are in your astral body you can pass right through physical things or people and they will be unaware of you. Also you must learn that there are many degrees of astral matter (or astral atoms), each functioning independently. In fact, there may be astral entities of a different speed of vibration from your own, walking through you at this moment!'

I started, violently. This was more than all my studies had divulged.

'Come! Come!' remonstrated Raphael. 'You know quite well that if you suddenly turned on a wireless set just by your elbow you would contact great volumes of sound from all over the world. Those sounds are there all the time and yet you otherwise hear nothing. The myriad waves flow through each other and yet each retains its separate existence. Does that teach you nothing? Cannot you conceive of creatures, spirits and entities, each carrying on his own life and activities while flowing through another life and oblivious to all else but his own sphere of vibrations?'

I stared at my companion almost angrily. I felt that he was trying my brain too hard. He only laughed at me.

'Why,' he exclaimed, 'there may be a planet passing straight through our earth at this moment, whilst we are oblivious of it because it is not wearing its physical body, but only, for the time being, its astral one.'

'Why are you tormenting me?' I asked in despair, my brain dizzily trying to grasp these strange ideas.

'No, I am not tormenting you, Verity!' soothed Raphael very gently, with that tender smile suddenly irradiating his luminous face and making me feel that I could follow him to the ends of the earth, 'but I am certainly tiring you. You see, you will have to begin using brain cells and brain muscles hitherto lying idle, and that is difficult work. Now it is time you slipped back into your body, thrusting yourself once more into the smothering, heavy pulsations of the flesh. I will not help you this time. You must learn to do it by yourself.'

Swaying gently over the floor I approached my body to consider the situation. But no sooner was I near to the divan than a violent sort of magnetic pull took place. With a swirl and a lurch which caught horribly at my middle, I was back in my body again. I panted anxiously feeling as if I had dropped from a height, a feeling which I suddenly recalled having experienced before, sometimes, in the night.

'Well, that wasn't so difficult!' I called out, rather proudly, as I opened my eyes.

But my friend was not to be seen.

'Raphael!' I called eagerly. But I was only answered by the empty silence, the cold moonlight and the dim but normal outlines of my room.

4

The Solar System

'Don't you think Bin might – you know what I mean – today, darling? Its going to be fine and warm!' said Marion next morning, when I appeared in her room all ready for gardening. I did know what she meant, of course. But Bin was learning so many words that one had to be careful. For instance it was not fair to mention either 'walk' or 'garden' in front of him unless those things were about to materialize for him, as he promptly worked himself up into a fever of excitement and anticipation. At present he was sitting bunched together in a position of the lions of Trafalgar Square, digesting his breakfast, with his eyes shut and his ears lying flat down.

'Yes, I was just going to suggest it – he can go part of the way by himself, and part of it in his Rolls Royce. Bin! Bin! Would you like to come for a *walkie* in the *garden?*'

Up shot Bin's ears, his eyes promptly bulged and his whiskers shook with excitement as he raced towards me and circled me eagerly, standing up on his hind legs, and begging to go. I took him up in my arms, thrilling to his warm, silky, quivering little body, and the relaxed and trusting way in which he thrust his head under my chin and made funny little noises of anticipation.

Marion came down to the front door to see us off. It was quite a procession. I pulled my little gardening cart from the outhouse, filled it with tools, and placed Bin on the ground in front of it. He glanced round to see that

all was ready, and then set off at a busy lope to lead me
to the walled garden, for hares must always lead, not
follow. It was quite a long route, past all sorts of fascinating flowerbeds, and patches of grass, right across the
court which flanked the old barn, and up to the gate of
the little orchard where the hens were kept.

Bin trotted proudly up to the gate and waited below
the latch, ready to squeeze through the instant I opened
it. Then he set off along the path to the walled garden,
looking behind at intervals to see if I and his Rolls Royce
were following. We called it his Rolls Royce because he
often rode in it, sitting amongst the tools with his head
presiding over the route we took. On the side of the Rolls
Royce was painted the word 'PerseVERAnce.' This had
been done by our former domestics, long since gone, who
had made the cart for me, in admiration of the keenness of
my gardening efforts. A robin, who was acquainted with
our daily procession, flew down onto the cart and explored
my gardening basket for the titbits which were usually
there. Then he flew on over the gate to wait by his little
broken cup, which I always left on the path for him and
replenished every morning. Bin lolloped up to the gate
of the walled garden and sat with quivering whiskers
whilst I unlocked it. Then he shot in, and knowing that
we had reached our destination, he took a flying leap
onto the earth and began to dig. The robin hopped round
him, fascinated, waiting for insects.

I wheeled my little cart round to my cabin, and flung
open the doors and went inside. The sun was quite warm
this morning and the earth would soon be dry enough for
sowing. I would have to plan it all out at once, because
the good weather was late this year. I took my gardening
magazines and set myself down to plot out the beds. My
autumn cabbage seedlings had weathered the winter and
were standing looking rather small and forlorn taking
their first sun-bath. I turned to 'cabbages' in my book,
and read: 'For cabbages, the following manures are men-

tioned by the Board of Agriculture: a) As growth com-
mences apply sulphate of ammonia, $\frac{1}{2}$ oz to a sq yd; b)
When cabbages refuse to "heart" use super-phosphate . . .'
What *were* those substances really, and what did they
actually *do?* Perhaps they were not the best and most
natural thing to use. Perhaps using them gave people all
the awful diseases they acquired so punctually. Animals
were diseased too – hens had so many diseases that it did
not do to think about them, if one were to continue eating
eggs. In nature there are not all those lumps of raw
chemicals lying about . . .

Oh dear, oh dear, here I was again, wondering instead
of working, I thought, as I jerked myself angrily back to
my job and started mapping out the seed-beds. The
broad beans and peas were of course already sown. The
next thing would be the salad beds, neat little rows of
lettuce, beetroot, radishes, and spring onions – oh, and
the small type of carrot to go with them. I knew this
whole procedure off by heart, even to the bordering of
the salad bed with an edging of charming crisp parsley.
It would take me all day to do the first sowing, and Bin
and I would have our fill of Mother Earth.

'Bin, where are you?' I called. Bin's gleaming white
head promptly shot up from behind the gooseberry bushes,
his nose and paws covered with delicious brown earth,
and his jaws champing happily at some long juicy root
he had discovered.

'O.K., Bin, this is the life!' I answered, and turned to
plunge my own fingers with rapture into the seed-bed.

I was lying on my divan that evening studying the seed
catalogue when I suddenly felt Raphael's presence. I
raised my eyes to discover him watching me. He was
outside the radius of my reading lamp, but its rosy glow
caught the glint of his curling beard and the twinkle in
his dark eyes. I wondered if perhaps he were an artist.

He was not wearing an ordinary man's suit, but a kind of dark smock which might have belonged to a painter, an artisan of some kind or even a priest. I leaned forward to look at him more closely.

'Oh no, you don't, my friend!' he laughed, stepping back swiftly into the shadow. 'I want you to concentrate on a much larger thing than myself tonight! I want you to begin to acquire a sense of proportion. So let us get to work. Will you kindly step out of your fleshly form!'

'I – er – all by myself? I don't think I can!' I stammered. Then, noticing the angry flash in my teachers' eye I quickly pulled myself together, and began to steady my breathing. I expected to feel the little wheels whirring inside me and sure enough they soon began to do so. Of course Raphael was helping me in his strange way, but, even so, I felt a sense of pride as I held myself steady whilst the revolvings grew rapid and strong and then swiftly reversed themselves inside me. One final wrench and I stood beside my companion. I realized that we were both in our smoky astral counterparts.

An overwhelming feeling of lightness and exhilaration took possession of me as I emerged out of the cramping prison of flesh. I looked back at my prone physical body and felt as a bird must feel when it is let out of a cage.

'So far, so good,' came Raphael's voice beside me. 'Now, are you ready for a very long journey?'

Hastily I looked round for my life-line. The little silver cord was shimmering quite strongly.

'Yes, I'm ready – oh, Raphael, yes, do teach me a sense of proportion, so that I can know which things really are important. I do worry a lot over little things.'

'Come, then, and do not be afraid.'

So saying, he leisurely left the surface of the floor and rose towards the ceiling. Anxious not to lose sight of him, I wished to follow and promptly found that I was doing so.

'What now?' I demanded excitedly as I hung just below the surface of the ceiling, feeling rather as if I were indeed a soap bubble.

'Follow me!' said Raphael and disappeared halfway through the ceiling.

'Wait – I can't do that!' I cried in amazement and alarm, swaying helplessly where I was.

'Why not? You're aura is half-way through already. Look closely and you will see me too.'

Sure enough the top of my beautiful surrounding bubble had gone ahead of me through the ceiling, while as I gazed I realized that I could still see Raphael, as if the solid surface were transparent.

'Oh, I'm sure my aura has been hurt!' I fussed. 'I can see some horrid dark yellow streaks in it!'

'That's only Fear. You've designed that pattern yourself! Of course we can go through the window if you prefer it, merely as a matter of form,' laughed Raphael.

'No, please give me your hand and pull me up – I simply can't get used to this!' I gasped anxiously.

Still chuckling, my kind friend grasped my smoky fingers in his. Together we floated gently upwards, nothing offering us any resistance. Soon we hung over the rooftops of my home, as they lay bathed in the soft brilliance of the clear moon. I looked down in astonishment at this new view of the Grange, every inch of which was evidently fully equipped with its smoky astral counterpart. It looked very much like a cinematograph picture, rather dim with age.

'Come along! Come along!' cried Raphael impatiently. I tore my gaze away and we floated steadily upwards, gaining speed as we went. I watched, entranced, as the beautiful moonlit panorama opened up beneath us. From time to time I glanced for reassurance at my life-line, which stretched steadily downwards like the string of a kite. I also peered for Raphael's life-line and was interested to see that it too, hung beside my own.

'Now then, no more peeping!' commanded my companion firmly. 'Why be so anxious about returning to that poor little carcase of yours? Surely it is nicer up here? Now I want you to watch everything carefully as we go.'

We must have been moving at incredible speed because already almost the whole of the countryside was visible to us, stretched out much like an ancient school map. The rivers could be seen plainly as their surfaces glittered in the moonlight. The towns could be located by the glint reflected from slate roofs, and the woods by the blackness of their inky depths.

'How beautiful!' I murmured to myself. To be suspended thus freely in the air was very different from being cooped up in the noisy restriction of a plane.

We were moving now with tremendous swiftness, as the atmosphere around us seemed to offer no resistance whatever. The rate at which the landscape was shrinking together beneath us was sufficient testimony.

'Can you see the etheric web yet?' asked Raphael. 'I am changing the focus of your eyesight so that it will become partly physical.'

I gazed intently at the country scene now in miniature below. Little by little I discovered an infinitely delicate silver tracery lying over the earth like a cobweb on an autumn morning. I held my breath with excitement, and peered for all I was worth. As my eyes accustomed themselves to the new focus, the web was more and more clearly visible, clustering thickly through the forest patches, running strongly with the rivers, fading out upon the roads.

'There's a break in the web,' I cried suddenly, 'just below us now!'

'Ah, yes,' said Raphael 'you're a good enough pupil when you try. That is a bomb crater. Sharp of you to see it! Now try and look *through*!'

'Through the earth?' I stammered, watching, however,

obediently. 'Why yes, I *can* see! The web does run through – right down – like it does through my own body! I see strange shapes, vague movements, patches of glowing light. Oh, Raphael, seeing the Earth this way it looks very much like my own physical form did! It makes me feel queer – almost frightened – of what I shall see next. Thank goodness we're getting too far away now for me to see any clearer!'

This was true, and even as I spoke the whole surface of the Earth gradually came into view. Soon it was hanging below us like a colossal ball of dull silver. It was patched here and there with what looked like large stains of iron. I saw that the silver was all ocean and the iron stains were the land.

'Yes, there is the physical body of our planet, the Earth! Can you still see its etheric double?' questioned Raphael gently.

'Oh yes, I can. It is like a blue phosphorescent light edging its round surface,' I whispered. Our voices were hushed because of the eerie magnificence of the scene. Far away on our left hung the moon, looking rather rigid and cold. It did not seem to palpitate with life like the Earth did, nor could I discern any etheric web around it. Like a great ball of roughened glass with a mirror surface, it threw back the rays of the hidden sun with blinding brilliance. Only as we left the moon behind were my eyes able to rest comfortably upon it.

'We are about to leave the surface of the Earth's aura, so you may feel a bit of a wrench. But keep right on!' came the steadying voice of my fellow traveller.

Even as I spoke I began to feel a sort of suction pulling at me, like a very strong draught. But I, who had marched airly through a ceiling and a tiled roof was not going to be intimidated by a bit of a gale. I pushed doggedly onwards, until suddenly the pull seemed to give way, and I was shot forwards like a pea out of a pod into silent vastness.

'Raphael! Raphael!' I called frantically. 'Where are you? I can't see you!'

'I'm here. You will soon learn to see me in this rarer atmosphere. Do not worry! Just follow me. Now look at the Earth's astral bubble.'

'What?' I asked incredulously, staring downwards nevertheless. The sight below me was glorious and unexpected. There hung the Earth growing rapidly smaller to our view, poised in the centre of a big beautiful iridescent bubble, like Raphael's and my own. Exquisite colours chased each other through and through this mysterious sphere, round and round upon its surface, intermingling with rapid wave-like movements. Seemingly dark against these airy colours, the Earth appeared to gaze through at us, like a sombre watchful eye.

'So the Earth has also an astral body! But – but – Raphael, you said astral stuff was the stuff of emotion and feelings!' I cried, with a faint hope of catching him out.

'Can you give me any reason why the Earth should not feel?' asked my companion quietly, winning the trick with one more of his unanswerable suggestions. I tried to change the subject.

'I can see some streaks of dark colour in the Earth's aura. Surely . . . surely that cannot mean faults of character?'

'All creations in the Universe are evolving to a higher state of perfection. But let us turn our eyes away. It is an impertinence for us so to scrutinize that great being.'

A surprising train of thought had been set up, however, and although I discreetly withdrew my glance my mind continued to speculate.

'You are quite right,' remarked Raphael, reading my thoughts, as it was becoming apparent that he easily did. 'Actually the trouble in the Earth's aura looks very much like that which I saw in your own aura just recently, due to your despair at the sickness and ignorance of your fellow men.'

'But – but – ' I stammered, 'that could not possibly mean that the Earth is also unhappy about humanity?'

By now I must have grown able to see Raphael fairly clearly again, because I turned after my question and found his eyes fixed upon me in what looked like grave approval, as if my struggles to comprehend exceeded his expectations. All he said, however, with that tantalizing abruptness of his was:

'Why not?'

'But that would be *quite* incredible!' I declared, almost angrily resentful at such an unaccustomed idea.

'My friend, there is really only one thing which I find incredible of all that I see – and that is the utter blindness of human ignorance.'

'Well, yes, we certainly do seem to be oblivious to everything but ourselves,' I agreed thoughtfully. 'To think how powerful the sufferings and emotions of a creature as big as the Earth *might* be – and to compare them with the troubles of a little human being!'

'Quite! A mere pin-point! I see that you have already learnt something of today's lesson, my friend, and that your sense of proportion is becoming slightly modified,' and he looked at me quizzically.

I returned his glance guiltily. I remembered how large my own troubles had always loomed. At present I could hardly call them to mind. Still, I *had* also worried about other people. I began to stammer excuses confusedly, but the twinkle in Raphael's eyes deepened, and I gave it up and broke into sudden laughter.

'May I ask you to attend once more to the matter in hand,' he demanded with mock gravity. 'You have had to come a long way to find your sense of humour, but there is further yet to go.'

'Further?' I echoed foolishly. 'But we seem to be at the end of the Universe already!'

'You are forgetting to use your eyes – and your wits. Remember that there are millions of stars visible to our feeble little telescopes alone. What about them? You seem to have overlooked them!'

'What? Are we going to visit a star?'

'No, not tonight. But how much do you know of Astronomy? What can you tell me of our solar system?'

'I know that it is a collection of planets; seven principal ones, I believe, and others less known, which all revolve round our Sun, each at its own special distance from the Sun, and the whole collection constitutes our solar system!'

'Not bad, for a woman! Do you know which is the planet nearest to the Sun?'

'Isn't it the tiny one, Mercury?'

'That's right! Now Verity, see if you can locate it.'

I looked downward and knew a thrill of suprise at the change of scene. It was difficult to remember how fast we were moving, when we could feel nothing either of effort or of speed. For a moment I could not pick out the Earth, for it was poised amongst a great cluster of other planets which had swung into view below us. In their midst was a burning ball of fire which I at once recognized as the Sun. I carefully studied the great star cluster. Finally I distinguished the Earth, because even at that distance I could still faintly decipher its outline of land and sea. Quite near to the Sun there was a very tiny and bright planet which I took to be Mercury. Then there was a larger one with a beautiful bluish tinge, another with a reddish glow, and further away, an orb which stood out by reason of its greenish colour. I had to look carefully, because all the space between these larger planets was speckled and spangled with smaller stars, some of them massed together, some of them gleaming still and stationary, and others with a swing of movement about them. All the same I could pick out the planets and also some of the little moons surrounding them.

'Have you found Mercury?' asked Raphael, 'and blue Venus? and red Mars? and green Saturn? Well done, Verity! Now look carefully, because I want you to imprint this scene upon your mind for ever. Do you notice any movement?'

'I know, of course, that all this system of stars revolves round the Sun in one direction, and I seem faintly to sense this great movement. Why, yes, Mercury has moved along even since I've been looking!'

'That is fine! You are becoming quite observant. Now, can you tell me where our solar system ends?'

'Ends?' I echoed doubtfully, gazing round at the vast expanse of the heavens which stretched endlessly away on all sides. Stars, stars, stars, millions and millions of them met my eyes in every direction. Great stars, little stars, brilliant or dull, poised alone or fused in crowds and groups together.

'No, how could anyone possibly tell where our solar system ends in the middle of all that?' I exclaimed. 'You expect too much of me, Raphael!'

'Be patient, my friend,' coaxed my Cicerone gently. 'There is a way of telling. Why not look for the etheric web of our solar system?'

'The web!' How could there be a web in the middle of the sky!' I expostulated. All the same I looked, carefully focusing my eyes as I had by now learnt to do.

Then I saw it. The scene below me gradually took on a strange and beautiful significance. At first I could dimly perceive a fine pulsating web of living electric strands, in which the stars were caught, like morning dewdrops on a cobweb. This web clasped them round like a gigantic woman's hairnet enclosing heavenly tresses, thus dividing a few hundred or thousand stars completely off from the rest of the Universe. In the middle of this colossal net glowed our little Sun, a globe of rich and gorgeous beauty. The Sun was the heart and centre of the cobweb, the very nucleus of it. For I saw that glowing filaments, tinted in the colours of the rainbow, spread out from its heart and linked up with the planets. I counted seven of these living rays, and was thus able to locate the seven major planets.

I saw that they gained their different tints from these filament rays, that they were nourished and fed with the
essence of life by the Sun itself.

Each planet in its turn radiated again seven coloured
rays, and these were divided and redivided amongst the
smaller stars until they spread into the finest electric cob-
webbing. Such a glorious vision it was, impossible fully
to describe.

'Seven sevens!' I whispered, as I remembered some of
the Ancient Wisdom teachings, and as I counted the art-
eries from sun to planets one again. 'Never will I forget
this scene. I did not know that such beauty existed, nor
such wondrous designs. I can see now what a complete
and separate whole our great star cluster is!'

'Seven is the number upon which our solar system is
planned. Do not forget it. Now we will go a little way
off and get a longer view,' remarked Raphael, once more
wearing the contented look which told me that I had
done well.

'A little way off must mean millions of miles,' I reflected
as we drew away from the vast net of stars until it hung
below us like a great shining jewelled globe. 'Can you still
see clearly?' asked Raphael, very quietly, waiting intently
for my answer.

I looked carefully. 'I can still see the surface pretty
well,' I muttered slowly. 'I cannot see through to the Sun
any more but I can see that the web goes through and
down – and I can see vague lights and movement beneath.
Why, merciful heavens, Raphael, it looks to me just as the
Earth did!! You're not going to tell me that the solar
system is a great body also?' I gasped, almost in despair.

Raphael smiled at me, lovingly, tenderly, and opened
his lips to speak.

'Yes, I know just what you're going to say – "*Why
not?*"' I interrupted him. ' "Why not?" "Why not?"
But how can one believe such incredible things – how *can*
one?'

'The seeker after the Truth,' began Raphael, 'must learn two things. He must learn to believe that anything and everything is possible – and he must never accept anything as the *final* Truth. Now let us go a little further.'

'Further – further where?' I asked, looking helplessly round.

'Further from our home – our solar system. Be patient, my friend, our journey is nearly done.'

As we drew rapidly away from the star-clustered web beneath us I felt rather forlorn. How long would it take us to get all that way back, if we ever did! My attention was soon caught, however, when I suddenly realized that we were gazing down upon *two* star-clustered webs! I blinked and looked again, but there they were!

'What is it – not another solar system surely?' I ventured.

'You've guessed right. And here is a third and a fourth, and yet another, all quite near to our own. Now look!'

Gradually we drew away from the beautiful balls of jewelled webbing as they hung beneath us. Soon I could not distinguish our own solar system from the others.

'Look behind!' commanded Raphael, 'and do not be startled!'

I looked down behind us and saw that we had moved over above a great golden star. The solar systems were now so small to our view that they looked like glowing planets. They were all swinging round in the orbit of the enormous golden star, which was evidently their sun.

'So our solar system is part of a greater solar system? Yes, I remember having heard that,' I murmured, overawed. 'But then – does that have its vast etheric web too?'

'Yes, my friend, in a way. But here we touch on mysteries too grand for our little conceptions. And you have worked quite enough for tonight. So we will now return home.'

'Just one more look!' I begged, gazing hungrily at the

weird beauty of those vast, orderly orbs beneath us as they stood out against the background of billions of stars dwarfed by distance and stretching into infinity on every side. At last I relaxed the tense focus of my vision. The etheric webs gradually faded from my view. I could see nothing but stars, stars, stars, of all sizes and inextricably mixed.

'Oh, Raphael!' I exclaimed with a deep sigh. 'Now the sky looks just as usual. I could almost disbelieve what I have seen. Could it possibly be that – that –.' I was afraid to finish.

'That I have been hypnotizing you?' came my friend's quiet voice. 'Well, I am glad that you are not too ready to be taken in. That is excellent. But no, Verity, all that you have seen is quite true – *up to a point*! Nevertheless it would have been possible for me to show you all that I have shown you tonight – but from *another angle* – and it would, in that case, have looked *very* different! Now you can digest that, as you want to know so much!'

I stared at him in bewilderment. 'Oh!' I breathed, 'I do wonder what it would –.'

'That's enough!' commanded my friend. 'I don't want you to crack your brains when we have barely started. There is such a thing as spiritual greed, you know. Now we are going home.'

'Oh! However are we going to get back? Are you sure you know the way?' I began to fuss.

'Ha, you have forgotten about your life-line at last, my nervous friend,' teased Raphael, 'and also that I told you that we can move faster than electricity. You only have to think of your body and you will be there.'

'My poor little body! It lies lost like the millionth part of a speck of dust in the midst of all that you have shown me. *So* insignificant! Yet it is my little home. I must hurry back and see if it is still safe – do come, Raphael!'

I felt a jerk and a pull as I started off, and then nothing more. I looked around. But I could see only darkness.

I knew an instant of terror.

'Raphael! Raphael!' I cried.

Then I perceived the square of my bedroom window blinking at me through the darkness.

Raphael was gone and I was back on Earth once more.

5

The Army Arrives

The next day some of the army turned up.

The Grange and its lawns were bordered by the main cross-road and a little village green. The main road led on towards Colchester and from thence to the coast. It seemed to be the route for most of the army in the district. On several occasions generals and majors had walked in with the intention of requisitioning the whole place. But they had reckoned without Marion, who used every tactic in woman's large repertoire to avoid our being set adrift upon the roads. It appeared that although generals might command armies they quailed before our little cousin when she was really on the war-path. Possibly they were also slightly confused by Bin's bushy quivering whiskers as he inspected one gigantic pair of boots after another. However it was, we had continually retained possession of our homestead, although encroachments were nevertheless made.

The Grange was painfully eligible as an army headquarters. Finally real pressure was brought to bear. A compromise was reached with a fierce and bewhiskered general, to requisition half the Grange and half its grounds, leaving us two ladies still entrenched in our own wing. The little room in which Marion elected to stay was at the top of the staircase, so that she commanded a full view of the comings and goings of all concerned.

Her window overlooked the inner courtyard where the

men were marshalled and paraded every morning, so what she did not know about the life of the regiments one way and another was not worth a cent. My own room was very much more secluded. As I was always too tired after gardening to do much fraternizing I left most of it to Marion. Her hospitable and motherly instincts were profoundly aroused by the presence of 'the men' under our roof. Rationing, alas, severely restricted her movements, but what she did manage was little short of a miracle. Endless cups of tea, bowls of soup, glasses of beer and smokes circulated mysteriously through the Grange, propelled by Marion, often surreptitiously evading the eagle eye of authority, but more often bumping straight into it. Marion was always quite sure that she could get away with murder, but I waited from day to day to hear that she had been court-martialled.

Of course I did not actually see much of what went on. I had my job up in the walled garden, army or no army. What the troops thought of the sight of Bin leading me and his cart solemnly through the grounds every morning has yet to be discovered. We often had to pass across the barn courtyard whilst drill was in progress, and we both did so with becoming dignity, wondering how much 'Eyes right' was being observed. Once safely locked inside the walled garden, however, we could relax, and run and bound over the spongy earth, to explore the new growth on every side. The little feathery delicate rows of carrots were already up. Bin sat down amongst them and began to sample one or two.

'Bin!' I instantly called, in the stern sharp voice which meant 'forbidden fruit', and clapped my hands. Bin crouched still and waited for me to forget. Then he surreptitiously began to nibble again. 'Bin! No! Naughty!' I called vigorously. Bin then realized that it was an irrevocable veto. Tossing his ears 'All right, I don't want your nasty carrots!' he lolloped away to find a more permissible pasture. He never touched the carrot bed again, and seemed remarkably quick to grasp which were weeds, or his perquisite, and which were the untouchables.

I had settled down, during the early days of April, to the exquisite satisfaction of sowing and planting, my mind's eye busy picturing the coming results. Here would be the parsnips, wide apart, growing very dignified with their long fronded leaves. And here the onions with their firm delicate spikes, the whole bed looking like a lady's green hairbrush. Here I would have a clump of nasturtium to brighten things up and to keep away the blight. Their pale round leaves, so good in salad, were a constant delight. And here would come the long rows of peas with their thin oval leaves and generously swelling pods.

Fronded, spiked, round, oval! All these varied shapes and scents and fruits. What did they mean? Why *were* these shapes? What was the meaning of *variety?* Such infinite variety, of taste, of smell, of shape, of colour! *Why?* One knew, of course, that certain herbs had certain curative properties. Sometimes one came across an old village character who would nod his head solemnly and pronounce old adages. One was inclined to dismiss them as 'superstitions', although it was admitted that there was often 'something in it!' But this was all very vague. What was the truth behind it all? Could one know perhaps by the shapes, any more about the herbs and plants than was already known?

Where was Raphael?

It was a week since my adventure in the sky, my dream-adventure, as it now seemed. The bustling advent of the army, filling the house with its comings and goings, night and day, had quite upset the steady rhythm of our lives, and had probably prevented my secret friend from reaching me again. Only the waning moon hanging above me in the mild April sky could bear witness to the strange and thrilling experience which we had shared. I looked up at its cold withdrawn face, turned away from me now as if in disdain. I dropped my tools and sank down upon the garden bench. What was I supposed to be thinking and feeling since that amazing voyage of instruction? Had it given me any of the knowledge for which I yearned? It was indeed wonderful to think of the ordered pattern, so vast and so beautiful, upon which the skies were built. But did that help one to cope with the terrible, pathetic helplessness of human affairs? As I had watched the soldiers tramping about, 'under orders', living in my home, so strange to them, far from their own homes, their wives, their jobs and their pals, knowing that a horrible fate was probably awaiting them, which would be due to circumstances about which they knew nothing, and had contributed less – told that they were to fight for freedom and justice, things about which they had only the woolliest ideas – as I had watched all this I had felt what futile little puppets all of us were. And if I chanced to remember my wondrous adventure it only made me feel all the more pigmy-like and at a loss.

My thoughts were interrupted by a familiar busy snuffling and scratching in the gooseberry bush behind me. Evidently Bin had just uncovered one of his favourite roots and was having an ecstatic time. He always knew exactly which roots and plants he desired to eat, and when he desired to eat them. He always enjoyed everything he ate with the keenest relish. He always proceeded to wash his face and paws very scrupulously after feeding, and he always finished by lying full length to digest his meal, giving happy little reminiscent chews. How did he unerringly single out just the weeds which suited him? He knew far more than human beings about these things. *How* did he know? The light was rapidly fading. It was time to go in. I got up from my seat, and Bin, instantly realizing that he was about to be disturbed, increased the tempo of his digging and chewing almost to a frenzy.

'I'm *so* sorry, Bin, but I'm afraid we're late – we *must* go!' I apologized as I plunged my arms into the prickly bush and took hold of his hot, panting, resisting little body. Out I pulled him at last, covered with earth, and hastily chewing at a long white root which dangled from his whiskers. He cuddled into my arms very forgivingly as I carried him, root and all, over to our little cart and deposited him in it, surrounded with all the gardening tools. He sat up and looked over the top as he rode in lordly fashion back to the Grange. A bird was singing exquisitely, telling the world of the nest he had begun to build that day – a nest with only bare twigs above it as yet. How did that bird *know* that it would be safely sheltered with leaves by the time his family needed it? How *did* he know?

'Is that you, Verity?' called Marion's voice from the drawing room as I went past. 'We have a visitor here, darling – oh, this is my cousin, Mrs Nibs – you must excuse her, she's on the land, you know, not a very tidy job!'

'Hah do yer do!' said Mrs Nibs loftily in her very ha-ha voice. She was our most important neighbour. 'I'm just telling Miss Marion about the evacuee scandal – you've no doubt heard? Its quite monstrous!'

'I'm afraid I haven't heard' I admitted apologetically as I sank into a chair, and noticed Marion's eyes were big and flashing.

'Well, everyone in the countryside is in a fine state about it. It's bad enough to have these shoals of evacuees dumped on us from the East End and heaven knows where, but no-one had any ideah what they were going to be like!'

'But the poor things have mostly been bombed out, haven't they? And I don't suppose they wanted to come, either!' I said.

'But the disgrace of it! I can see you don't know! My deah, they are simply *infested* with vermin! Simply infested! *And* vermin of all kinds, mind you! Kinds that we don't mention!'

'Yes, I went to a lecture once in London,' I remarked artlessly, 'it was all about bugs, and the lecturer explained that it was not much good trying to give the poor people extra milk and what-not, so long as their blood was being steadily drained away . . . '

'Verity! Please!' expostulated Marion, horrified. 'Mrs Nibs, my cousin is an artist . . . ' she apologized, as if that evidently covered a multitude of sins.

'Well, Marion, its just because nobody wants to face these things that they exist. Its not the poor people's fault, you know, its the kind of houses they are forced to live in!'

'Yes, my deah, but there are other things besides – worse things!' interrupted Mrs Nibs, her eyes bulging with excitement, determined to get on with her bit of scandal. 'It appears that the children, some of them, have never been taught to – er – use the lavatory, and they – er – well, really, I – er – hardly can bring myself to tell you,' she exclaimed, getting all ready to do so, 'but it seems that they – er – use the *walls* my deah, the drawing-room walls, in some cases!'

'Yes, I understand they believe that this kills those certain insects!' I exclaimed, before I could help myself. 'Poor, poor things, just fancy that – that is their only hope!'

Marion gasped and hastily got up to offer cigarettes or in some way change the conversation, whilst Mrs Nibs gaped very disapprovingly at the uncouth land-girl and began to collect her reticule and other belongings.

'Well, well! I came to warn you both! You have a big house here – lots of empty rooms. I was afraid they might be commandered for evacuees! I didn't realize the troops were already here! Miss Marion has not managed so badly for herself, I see!'

Leaving us to digest this parting thrust and decide what it might mean, Mrs Nibs took her departure in correct style, whilst I slipped hastily upstairs to have my bath

before Marion could start telling me what she thought of
me.

'Bin, I think you will have to stay in the hen-run this
morning,' I announced to my fellow gardener one morning
towards the end of April. 'I am going to wander all around
today to look at the fruit trees – the buds are wonderful!'

We had come to a halt in the little orchard, where the
hens were kept in their big wire-netting run under the
Bramley apple trees. It was glittering spring weather,
the sun glinting on a world wet with gentle rain. The
Bramley buds were like bright coral beads and the old
trees appeared to have decked themselves out in neck-
laces. The hens were clucking happily over their morning
mash which I had just poured into their tin bowls. They
were too occupied for the moment to notice Bin, who
rushed willingly through the door of the hen-run directly
I opened it, and careered around to stretch his legs, tossing his ears delightedly and giving high goat-like leaps in
the air in his appreciation of the new sunshine. I was
reluctant to leave this delightful scene, but I took my sec-
ateurs out of the 'Rolls Royce' and began to wend my
way through the big orchard to do some trimming and
pruning. The orchard appeared to be sprayed with a
feathery green powder, so rapidly were the buds burgeon-
ing and bursting on every hand. In between the rows of
plum and apple and pear trees were regiments of gooseberry and currant bushes. At the end were an overgrown
asparagus bed and a strawberry bed swathed in grass. I
looked rather hopelessly at it all. In a few weeks an up-
rush of weeds, brambles and stinging nettles would begin
amongst all this lovely potential fruit and there was nobody
to stop it. By June the weeds would have become a
jungle, by July a forest! The grounds were big enough to
keep four gardeners busy. It was as much as I could do
to keep the walled garden, the little orchard and the front

garden going. So the big orchard had to be left to its own devices. The result was picturesque in the extreme, but enough to fill a good gardener with horror.

I snipped and chopped and tugged and tidied all morning until I was going up in steam, and then I came back to pick up Bin on the way in to lunch. I approached the hen-run quietly and soon realized that a drama was building up. Bin was sitting cleaning the damp mud off his whiskers and ears for dear life, making quite loud snortling noises of busyness as he worked. Beside him sat the big speckled hen, her feathers puffed out, looking at him most coquettishly out of the corner of her eye, and edging every few minutes nearer and nearer. It was plain that she thought him a demi-god possible of seduction. It was plain, not only to me, but also to her legal lord, the Leghorn cock, who was starting to do a war-dance just behind them, and working himself up for a tremendous attack in defence of wifely rectitude.

Meanwhile Bin remained serenely indifferent – or apparently so, for who could tell how much· Bin could see? His eyes looked out on each side of his head, so he saw twice as much as a human being does, anyway. But could he see a bit in front or behind as well? One was convinced that he did a lot of seeing with his whiskers, but the cock wondered also if he could see with his magnificent long ears. He was a game little cock, and he was making one or two fine rehearsals of his coming attack. I suddenly had a moment of terror.

Would the cock attack Bin fiercely and scratch out his eyes? Before I could move the white bird launched himself upon my little friend's sleek and unprotected white back.

But I had reckoned without Bin. I might have known! In a flash he turned and said 'Boo!' to the cock – just like that! Suddenly the long pink ears, the bulging pink eyes and the bush of quivering whiskers were thrust into the cock's very beak. It was too much for my lord. With a squawk of astonished horror he leaped into the air and almost turned a somersault. Then he bolted without any dignity, and tried to pretend he had not been there at all – a really terrible position for the master of the roost.

Bin tossed his ears, turned his back on the hen whose heart was all of a flutter, and calmly resumed his toilet.

I decided I really need not worry about him.

When finally he saw me coming he crouched flat down, waiting to be picked up. He relaxed his hot, joyous little body across my shoulder and chattered in my ear of all the morning's doings.

Why was there such a special ecstasy in friendship with an animal?

6

Inside the Atom

That night I realized that I was not going to be able to sleep. Long after all the soldiers' noises had died down I was lying with wide open eyes. I was thinking of Mrs Nibs' stories of the poor evacuees. How was it possible that in this much-vaunted twentieth century, the British people with all their missionaries in all the backward corners of the earth, permitted such ways of living, in *London* – the hub of the universe! For there were other tales whispered which I did not even want to think about or remember. Those slum districts were surrounded with churches, with County Councils, with Women's Institutes. What were they all doing? It certainly was a good example of being 'half alive'! I tossed and tossed, thinking of those poor people, inured to conditions that would demoralize any animal.

Finally, I sat up, panting with distress.

Moonlight was flooding the room and Raphael was standing watching me. 'Oh! You!' I gasped. 'I wondered if you were ever coming again!'

'When you need me,' he answered quietly, 'I come!'

I did not know what to answer. The experiences that I had had with him were wonderful – but my need was not for adventures – my need was for some way in which to *help*. Nothing else mattered.

'Come along out, my friend!' said Raphael, nodding at me gently.

I was just beginning to long to taste the almost-forgotten

freedom once again, when with a sudden swirl I found that I had left my body and was by his side.

'Well, and how do you feel about things after our last full moon's adventures?' he asked interestedly.

I looked into his charming, familiar face. A deep affection was growing for him in my heart. I hated to be disappointing.

But to him one could not lie.

'I feel dreadful!' I burst out bluntly. 'You have shown me marvellous sights! You have expanded my conception of the Universe beyond belief. And the more you have shown me of those vast lives the more utterly, minutely insignificant and feeble do *I* seem, seen thus in true perspective. A man is, after all, merely a microbe, one of millions upon a planet which is itself only one of millions! You have certainly changed my sense of proportion. I can no longer take seriously the troubles of such a microbe as myself – I can no longer be interested in her at all! Of what importance, of what use can she possibly be? In realizing my utter insignificance I have lost the will to live and to do! My former desire to be of use in the world seems to me now like the waving of the antennae of an ambitious ant. I feel crushed and of no account.'

Tears of self-pity were not far off.

'My poor Verity!' said Raphael sympathetically, 'I know how you feel. That is quite a normal reaction when you have only seen one side of the picture. You see how true it is that a little knowledge is dangerous. Reserve your judgment, I pray of you, until I have shown you some more. Now, our next experiment is going to make you feel rather strange. We are going to shrink!'

'Are you a magician, Raphael?' I asked him suddenly. 'How can you bring these things about?'

'My dear friend, if I were to say that I *am* a magician – what then? What would that convey to you? – absolutely nothing at all!' exclaimed my evasive companion. 'When we are in our astral bodies we are not limited by time, space or size. That is all I can say at present. But I want you to learn more about the relative importance of a human being. To do this we must enter a human body, and examine it thoroughly, so we must become small enough to do this comfortably. I will not take you into your own body, because it is asleep and I want you to study a conscious person. So we will explore one of your army visitors – I believe we will find the young regimental doctor studying his work downstairs. He will do nicely. Now follow me!'

I moved after him carefully. When he came to the closed door of my room he passed straight through it. I remembered my adventure with the ceiling, and putting my head down I bravely butted into the door. There might have been nothing there at all, for I sprawled through with great lack of dignity and nearly lost my balance. Raphael pretended not to notice, but I could sense his secret chuckle.

'Just give me a little more time,' I said, rather hurt, 'and I'll show you!'

Leisurely we glided rather than walked along the corridor, past Marion's open doorway and down the stairs. The door of the dining-room which was now used as the Officers' Mess, was open, and sure enough there was the young doctor, sitting all by himself, poring over his books.

As we advanced into the room he looked up and took off his spectacles. I thought he was about to speak to us and I opened my mouth in greeting. I was stopped by my companion's warning hand, and I then realized that the doctor was looking straight through us at the door and that he could not see us at all.

'Tut tut! Where can that draught be coming from!' he muttered with a slight shiver, as he replaced his spectacles and settled down to his work again.

'You can talk to me,' said Raphael, 'he will not hear us. Now we are going to shrink.'

No sooner had he said this than I felt a strange sensation. The doctor, his chair, the room, seemed to swell and grow rapidly larger. I recalled having experienced the sensation often before in my childhood, during a nightmare. But I had no time to consider this because the doctor's head was already towering far above us. Soon his knees passed swiftly upwards past my head. He seemed to have become a mountain of a man. His great bare foot in its felt slipper soon lorded it over us, becoming more than twice our height. I turned in amazement to Raphael who stood beside me seemingly unchanged.

'We have shrunk until we are only one inch in height,' he explained, 'but that is only a beginning. How would you like to remain always this size?'

I gazed around me. Everything looked completely strange. A network of great ropes fell down to the floor at my side. I realized that it was the edge of the doctor's woollen dressing-gown. From underneath it protruded an enormously thick blanket which I also concluded must be the edge of his pyjamas. His slipper seemed like a large cart. The very ground on which we stood was so full of bumps, splinters and hollows that I hesitated to move. Through the air floated a multitude of odds and ends, great pieces of cord and slabs of cardboard which turned over and over, catching the electric light as they moved.

'What are all these great things?' I asked, ducking to avoid one.'

'Only dust!' laughed Raphael. Now let us explore the doctor's foot.'

He rose upwards in the air as he spoke, and I promptly followed him. We landed gently upon the great coloured expanse of the young man's foot. It was very interesting to see the pattern of a human skin from such close quarters. It seemed to be laid out in large triangular slabs, punctuated by little holes, and all linked by criss-cross furrows. Hot steamy air was puffing gently out of the little holes, so that I had the impression of standing upon a centrally-heated floor of crazy-paving. As these paving-stones were growing rapidly larger I realized that we had begun to shrink again.

Soon I noticed large plants like sugar canes growing up at intervals near the holes.

'Hairs!' explained Raphael. 'But we are going to study smaller things today so we must shrink more quickly – are you ready?'

I nodded assent reluctantly, because I was extremely interested in the doctor's epidermis. However, the sugar canes swelled swiftly to enormous jungle trees, whose tops were quite out of sight. The ridges and furrows in the crazy-paving grew into steep rocks and deep trenches, so that we could no longer see for more than a few yards ahead. Before us yawned a large cavern from which poured a continuous current of hot air.

'This is one of the pores of the skin,' explained Raphael. 'I think we will go in here.'

I followed him down this tubular corridor in wondering silence, fascinated by the precision of the architecture of this tunnel, whose walls were covered with beautifully arranged slabs divided by bands of rubber-like substance. The walls were stretching and shrinking with curious rippling movements which reminded me of a snake. Just below this wonderfully-built surface I could see that a variety of large pipelines were laid down. They seemed to be of various colours and thicknesses.

'Raphael!' I asked in a whisper which echoed up and down the tunnel. 'What are those pipes for?'

'They are veins, nerves, oil ducts and muscle fibres,' replied my friend, watching my interested face, 'and I want you to remember that today your eyes are focused mainly on physical matter, because thus it is easier for you to understand today's lesson.'

'All this – in a single pore of the human skin!' I gasped. 'How infinitely complicated is life! But we are still shrinking very quickly,' I broke off, noticing that the tunnel had already swelled to the proportions of a lofty cathedral, its roof lost in the distance. We were now standing balanced upon enormous ridges, as the surfaces of the slabs were ribbed. Colossal crystal balls rolled through the air, jostling each other as they went. There was a strong but pleasant smell of chemicals.

'Those great globes are particles of water vapour which are escaping through this pore,' explained Ráphael, 'but we shall soon be small enough to see the actual cells which form these tissues. I am sorry that there is no time to-day to stay this size any longer, but we still have far to go.'

I perceived that Raphael spoke of our rapid change of size as if we were travelling. Indeed, there was some sense in this, because the spaces we had traversed while remaining in one spot seemed vast. I could not see the tunnel around us any more, because it had become too big, and there were such a lot of great obstacles obscuring the view. To my horror I now saw an enormous living creature struggling by. Great wriggling centipedes were swept along, things which looked like octopuses, also squirmy serpents. Suddenly I caught sight of a giant tadpole swishing his tail and coming straight at us.

With a cry I clutched Raphael. He held my shoulder firmly and laughed.

'You have forgotten that we are in our astral forms,' he said, 'and that physical matter cannot affect us. These great creatures are only microbes.'

By this time the tadpole was right on top of us. He was about the size of a large seal. He swam straight through us in angry haste, entirely oblivious of our existence.

'The cut direct!' smiled my companion, whilst I tried to recover my dignity. 'Now we are getting small enough to see the cells. Do you remember where you are, by the way?'

'On . . . on the doctor's foot,' I faltered, as a colossal

eel about twenty feet long squirmed its way between a dozen enormous crystal globes.

'And do you know what he is doing? He is tiptoeing (and I mean the doctor, not the eel) past your room on his way to bed. Little does he dream where you *really* are! But now let us look at these cells.'

By this time I could see that the uneven surfaces upon which we were balancing were composed of great balls about ten feet across, covered with a tough webbed skin of elastic fibre. These balls were packed cleverly together, the spaces between being filled with a looser webbing of rubber-like material. Enormous globules, some red, some white, and some transparent, slipped in and out of the meshes of the webbing, together with various strange, busy-looking, living creatures. I knew at once that I was looking at the blood-stream, with its red and white corpuscles and its phagocytes, and that I was watching air – oxygen and other necessities – being passed in and out amongst the cells. I could have remained for a long time gazing at the spectacle, but unfortunately Raphael was in a hurry.

'We still have so much to see today,' he apologized. 'Now let us look for the etheric double, please!'

As I focused my eyes the scene quickly changed to one of far greater beauty. The delicate phosphorescent blue webbing of electric wires became apparent, threading through the rubber fibres, spreading over the walls of the cells, pulsing through the white phagocytes and shimmering over the red globules of blood, like the bloom on a purple grape. It was as if the whole busy scene was intricately lit up with neon lighting.

'And so it is, in a way!' Raphael answered my thoughts. 'But these electric currents are also feeding the whole body with a variety of forces drawn from the ethers of the atmosphere, and of which you know nothing as yet. But you are now looking upon the secret of Life, the way in which a human being or any living creature or plant

Discussion with a cell

draws energy from the air, so that it can strive and grow and move, using a total of energy which could not possibly be stored within its own body. Now, see if you can look *through* one of the cells.'

'Yes, I can,' I replied slowly. 'I can see the etheric web running through – and down – I can see faint lights within, and movements – why, Raphael' I interrupted myself, 'I seem to remember saying those same words several times before?' and I looked at him anxiously.

There was a flash of that contented look across my friend's face which warmed me with a glow of pride.

'That is so, Verity,' he said. 'You used just those words when you first looked upon the etheric web of your own sleeping body, and again when you looked – "etherically" as we say – upon our Earth, and yet again when you gazed with that same focus upon our solar system and saw it as one corporate whole. There are a few sayings, great passwords to knowledge, which have been handed down since man was upon the Earth. One of them is: *"as above, so below"*!'

'As above, so below! I suppose that means that everything celestial repeats itself on Earth ad infinitum. I had heard of that saying, but the words convey little until one sees them in action as it were.'

'Yes, and in man's own body is detailed the whole plan, workings, and evolution of the Universe – as in a tiny mirror. That is why the Ancients said "Man know thyself!" Now I think we will shrink a little more and explore a cell.'

I watched expectantly as the great roundish cells swelled upwards until we could only see the one nearest to us, which lay like a giant barrage balloon, shackled to the ground and to its neighbours by a tangle of jungle-like rubbery tree-trunks. We passed between this forest of gleaming, shifting trunks and entered the cell through one of the cavernous openings which pierced its sides. It seemed like entering a great domed Olympia, into whose interior was packed an amount of varied activity and a large number of strange forms.

All the space in this big dome was packed with globules which seemed to be of various substances, although mostly transparent. These globules slid over and between each other like living balloons, some of them apparently in a great hurry to get somewhere, others content to drift and be pushed aside. I remember the substance, half jelly half liquid, which scientists describe as filling the interior of a cell, and concluded that at the size we were now, each globule might be a molecule of liquid.

'To what height have we shrunk, Raphael?' I queried, peering up at the lofty dome overhead.

'This cell is less than one five-hundredth of an inch high! Reckon it out for yourself!' was the smiling reply. I did not feel equal to that effort, so I followed behind my friend as we explored further into the cell. We passed long enormous sausage-shaped creatures which swelled and curved and appeared to be full of life. There were also great round bodies with speckled surfaces, and smaller beautiful ones like jelly-fish. Tubes and strands of all sizes threaded their way in and out. Finally we approached a large collection of big banana-shaped creatures curled around each other tightly. In between them nestled solid-looking globes of pink, dark red and brown.

'This must be the nucleus of the cell!' I exclaimed, gazing at this closely-packed crowd, who were all possessed of delicately shimmering movement, almost as if they were breathing.

'Yes, Verity, here we are before the heart and mind of this great cell. Scientists have already declared that each cell has its own individuality, its separate consciousness, that it is either discriminative, greedy, quarrelsome, affectionate or well-disciplined as the case may be. Would you like to talk to this cell – ask him any questions?'

'Are you joking?' I replied, rather hurt. 'You're not going to tell me that this cell can talk? And whatever should I ask it anyway?' I was almost sulky with incredulity.

'Speech and words are not the only forms of conversation, as you, who have been studying bird and animal life so carefully, know. Even in human telepathy, which works like lightning, words as we know them, are not used. I am able, through long practice, to read the language of most creatures, and I can interpret to you the consciousness of this cell in respect of your questions. Ask them!'

'What an amazing man you are, Raphael! It is hard to believe you! All the same I should like to know what ambitions this cell possesses, what he believes in, and what part he thinks himself to be playing in the general scheme of things?'

Raphael stood fixed at attention for a while. In spite of myself I was distinctly conscious of some interplay between him and the great nucleus before us. Finally he spoke.

'The cell says: I am quite an old cell; the parent of many who surround me. I have done my best to imbue my children with the highest ideals and the most worthy and devout habits. My ambition is to leave behind as fine a group of well-trained cells as I can, to carry on the work of evolution. I believe, of course, in our divine Creator, in whom we live and move and have our being. We are all part of the body of this divine Being whose mind and life it is impossible for us tiny ones to visualize. He depends upon our discipline and well-being for His own well-being and development. If we worship Him and obey His demands implicitly we shall in time become initiated, so that we shall eventually share in the wonders of His mind.'

'Who is this god – this great deity?' I demanded.

'That is a forbidden question for the cell,' whispered Raphael to me, 'but you know him – it is the young doctor!'

I was beside myself with interest. 'Are you content to be a cell?' I asked, addressing myself directly to the nucleus, and entirely forgetting my erstwhile scepticism.

The clustering bodies shivered as I spoke and I could have sworn it was in eagerness to answer me.

'We cells are always striving for something better,' translated Raphael slowly, 'so there is sometimes jealousy. Our Creator sends to us all that we need, yet some of us are too greedy or too lazy – and that upsets the balance of our community and then disease and death appear. We are jealous of our rival communities. The cells of the liver are as foreigners to the cells of the heart, for instance – and although our Creator is always trying to impress upon us that we are all one family, it doesn't make much difference. Cell-nature doesn't change, you know! There will always be strife! Sometimes supply and demand are unequal so economical disturbances abound. We do not seem able to learn that lesson of universal cell brotherhood. Sometimes we blame our Creator for our troubles, and we feel sure that He sometimes blames us. The highest ambition of every cell is that after his death he or she may be reincarnated in the cell community of the brain. Those are what we call the grey races, the most highly civilized of us all!'

The nucleus was by now in an obvious state of excitement, and I felt that in a little while I should hardly need an interpreter at all.

Raphael, however, drew me away quietly, and I saw that he was sunk in deep thought.

'I wish I could describe to you,' he said at length, 'all that was then disclosed. There is so much to learn here. We should have to come here again and again. But now we must go on. I want to show you the inside of an atom. Each of these molecules of liquid is made up of innumerable atoms. Yes, I think this one will do.'

We paused in front of a large transparent globule, and by the quick speed at which it swelled before us, I knew that we were shrinking again. Soon we passed within this molecule, which had become so big that I could no longer see its walls. Around us there seemed to be nothing but pulsating space, in which I could feel an enormous energy like that of electricity of very high voltage. Every now and then there was a tremendous pull as if of some great invisible magnet. The air surrounding us took on a bluish tinge and the distant walls of the molecule looked like nothing so much as a blue sky.

'We have now passed within one of the atoms,' explained Raphael, 'but we shall have to get a million times smaller before we can see anything. So we will now shrink extra quickly.'

We floated freely through the blue universe, interrupted at intervals by those strong, intermittent magnetic currents. Presently I became aware of something gleaming ahead of us. It was a fiery little ball, poised in the midst of space, and it looked very like the Sun.

'Is that the nucleus of the atom – the proton? How very tiny it is!' I remarked looking around at the blue expanse of hemisphere. A large revolving electric spark flashed vividly by, and there was another further away.

'Can those be electrons – how frightfully quickly they move!' I exclaimed, fascinated.

'That depends on our size,' replied Raphael. 'The smaller we become the slower will they appear to move.'

'Yes, already they are beginning to look like little planets spinning – and the sun is glorious! I can hardly believe that I am not sailing with you under our own familiar sky as we did on our first night's journey.'

Indeed, by now the electrons looked like large fiery globes. I could see that they were each spinning around in their own orbits. One of them seemed to be of a distinct green shade and this gave me a sudden inspiration. I carefully focused my eyes for the etheric web. For a little while I could detect nothing. Then gradually the significance of the scene deepened before me and the etheric web appeared. First of all I saw delicate rainbow-coloured strands reaching out from the heart of the sun and linked to the little planet-electrons, from whom they passed again as finely divided webs of shimmering light. I watched closely.

'How can those strands remain linked with such quickly-moving bodies without becoming mixed up or confused?' I asked at last.

'Think of your own life-line!' replied Raphael, 'on our last journey we passed thousands of fellow travellers like ourselves and no confusion occurred. You did not see them because you are only learning to see by degrees. Think how all the *sound* waves remain intact until they are selected by the radio receiver! Millions of different waves flow through each other without becoming mixed. And as for the speed of those electrons – if our solar system were to appear to us the size of an atom, how fast would its planets seem to be moving?'

By this time we were approaching quite near to the radiant sun upon which I could hardly bear to look. It quivered and gleamed and glowed with such vivid compressed life, such shimmering vital movement that I was almost afraid to face it.

'Are we – are we going into that sun?' I faltered.

'No, Verity, that sun is the heart of life, the same as our own Sun, and contains forces and secrets too powerful for us to contact at present. Even our scientists suspect the extent of the deeper force still locked within the atom, and its ever more complicated contents. Our journey is over for today. Take your last look before we return home.'

Raphael's voice sounded very tired, and I looked at him with concern.

'Isn't it a great effort for you to show me all this? Why do you take so much trouble just for me?' I asked humbly.

'My fate and yours are bound up together,' replied my

companion gravely. 'For long ages I have waited for you, waited and prayed for this hour. You will understand why later on. But now tell me how you liked this journey?'

I gazed around at the blue distance, the shining sun, the glittering planets, almost unable to find words.

'I am filled with a vast amount of speculation. My mind is so full that I can hardly think. But I am aching to know more. What, for instance, do those seven colours *mean* which stream from the sun of our solar system, and ray out again from the nucleus of a tiny atom?'

'As above, so below!' reminded my guide. 'Colour holds a great number of secrets. Those who truly understand colour hold the key to wisdom. What else have you noticed, Verity?'

'It is difficult to put into words, Raphael, but I have watched all the ordered growth and planning which you have shown me, all the hurrying purposeful life, each globule, each molecule, each microbe, each corpuscle seeming to be driven by a purpose. How do they all know what to do?'

'Your observations are wise, my friend,' said Raphael as the contented look I loved so much appeared on his face. 'So far I have only shown you the outer physical coating of things, the expression and effects of inner causes. One day you shall see the inner causes for yourself. You shall see a world, a host of living beings, workers of all grades and sizes, who each have their task of ministering to and guiding and teaching physical creatures. Knowledge of them is veiled to us at *present*, but it used to be expressed in folklore and myth. One day you will learn something of this numerous host, from the Cherubim, Seraphim and all the Company of Heaven, to the fairies, the undines, gnomes and pixies!'

I did not laugh at these words. I had already seen too many marvels. I held my peace, gazing my fill upon the scene and murmuring quietly to myself: 'So this great solar system of light and splendour is but the inside of an atom, of one molecule, in one cell, in the tissue of the foot of our army doctor!'

'Yes, my dear, you have seen but one finite fraction of all the various living, growing, striving, conscious beings who depend utterly for their safety and progress upon the intelligence and behaviour of their Creator and deity, that young doctor. Thus from one angle, do you see the importance of a human being?'

'Ah, you mean that I, for instance, am actually responsible for all such lives within me?'

'My friend, did you not create them? Did you not help them to become what they are, and is it not for you to inspire them that they fulfil your needs and work with and not against you?'

'You mean – that there could be conscious mental interplay between me and all the lives in my own body?'

'Exactly, Verity, in that way can a human being become omnipotent and learn to do and be anything that he wishes. To be a god one has first to know oneself as a god and then to behave as one!'

I broke into bewildered laughter.

'Ha ha, on our first journey I learnt that I was less than a speck of dust! Today you show me to myself as a god, ruling millions and millions of lives! Whatever is the purpose of it all? Raphael, what is the purpose of it all?'

But the violence of my laughter seemed to have disturbed things somewhat. For everything had grown suddenly dark. I looked anxiously round for the sun and the planets, but saw instead only the square of my bedroom window. And I was alone once more.

7

Bin Acquires a Wife

As life all around us blossomed and budded with richness and freshness and ceaseless energy, it seemed to me as if I were seeing it all for the first time. Where had I been during all my previous springs? Evidently, I also had been only half alive like the rest. Never had I noticed how clear and glorious was the colour of the fresh green grass, how intricate and varied the designs of the hundreds of different wild plants, hitherto dismissed carelessly just as 'weeds'.

As I watched Bin munching eagerly, selecting this and that, searching out different flavours which meant so much to him: as I noticed various birds, so little known to me, carrying on their busy work, finding and choosing myriads of tiny things which I could not perceive at all: as I saw the majestic beauty of one tree after another putting forth its wealth of fresh blossom, breathing forth sweet fragrance, enchanting the scene, each with its unique form: as all this burgeoned about me day after day I was overcome. My heart was too full. I did not know how to contain my response to it all. I felt that hitherto I, an artist, had always looked without seeing, stared without perceiving.

And why this change now? Was it because for the time being my busy rush for career-making and money-earning had been cut short? Or was it because I had been shown the pulsating intensive life which in such an individual manner was permeating through everything? I could not look at a bird or a blade of grass now without imagining the luminous etheric double, its quivering astral aura, the packed consciousness of its teeming cells. Was Bin a little 'lord' to all his cells? He certainly seemed to know how to treat his body better than most human beings do.

I put up my spade and flung myself face downwards on the grass, pressing my face into its cool brilliance. I wanted to dream. Up against my cheek a strong blade of green pressed, tickling me. I squinted at it. It was cover-ed with a fine down of fluffy minute, up-standing hairs. I remembered how such hairs had looked to me as I prepared to take my voyage down the cavernous pore which they sheltered.

Suddenly there was a plop, and a grasshopper landed upon the blade of grass. I kept quite still. The insect sat stiffly up and worked his back legs energetically to emit his curious hissing call. What strange language was that, I wondered, and what did it mean to those who could translate it?

The little fellow broke off a tasty morsel of grass with his tiny hands and began to eat, chewing with his wide firm mouth whilst his keen eyes searched his horizon appreciatively. How strange a little man he was! His meal finished, he washed his face, just as scrupulously as did Bin, and then with a sudden leap disappeared through the air, to recommence his busy chirruping a little further off.

Up in the blue sky a lark was singing, twittering up-wards in lonely ecstasy. Nearby the bees were humming, amazed at the sudden appearance of their bounty of blossom. I listened to all the lovely sounds, the larks, the grasshopper, the bees, my clucking hens, the blackbirds and finches and Bin's particular little rapturous notes. It all made a subtle and fascinating orchestra.

Then, cutting right across it the siren suddenly began its wail, sad and clear and not unbeautiful, echoed by its fellows right across the unspoilt countryside. I did not stir. I had become too entranced. Soon a German bomber sailed rapidly across the pure blue sky, then another. There followed the booming sound of several falling bombs, and the sharp noise of gunfire. Then once more unbroken silence until the sirens sounded the 'All Clear'.

Somewhere within walking distance, death, agony and bereavement had rained suddenly down on harmless people intent only upon running their little homes. The lark was still singing, bees and hens continued their life unconcerned and unaware. Only little Bin had noticed. He had rushed quickly to my side and tucked his head under the hollow of my arm for safety. For *he* had been through the war in China. And evidently hares, like elephants, do not forget.

The days lengthened and spring was soon in full flow. The gorgeous tulip tree had long since scattered her beautiful cups. The fascinating chestnut leaves had opened their little hands and the blossoms had fulfilled their intricate patterns upon the scented air. The pink spearheads of their flowers had pointed proudly upwards, whilst their beauty was challenged by the golden torrents of laburnum blossoms as they poured down like rain from heaven. The rich clusters of azaleas, the clouds of purple lilac, the starry carpets of daises – all had come forth at their appointed time, each with its own particular expression of beauty, of colour, of form and of scent. Their flowers had flung out enticements to bees and moths and butterflies in order to achieve their mating. The enthralled insects had carried the pollen, and fruiting time had already begun.

I could see the baby chestnuts beginning to swell, and the tiny gooseberries suddenly appearing. I could hear the elfin squeaks of the young birds clamouring for food in their nests. On every hand were signs of mating and fruiting and of new living things.

One of my hens went 'broody' and we had to get her a clutch of eggs. She made a very special little purring sound as she settled herself down over her new possessions and went into a trance of satisfaction.

The family wrote that Bin ought to be given a wife. 'Get him an Angora rabbit if you can' was the advice. 'Although he is a hare and Angoras are small and rather stupid, he's quite foolish about them and loses his heart completely.'

I finally discovered a young woman in the next village who bred Angora rabbits. She promised to bring us the finest lady of all, to do honour to Bin. She cycled over one day with Bin's affianced swinging in a basket from the handlebar.

We were impressed when we first beheld Fluffy, as she was called. Indeed she was just an enormous ball of white fluff with two frightened eyes and a pair of ears with white fur tassels on the tips. We put her in the stable with her newly-prepared haybox and with much trepidation we let Bin in through the door.

Marion and I clutched each other anxiously outside. Would Bin kill Fluffy, would Fluffy scratch out Bin's eyes, what would happen between these nervous strangers? Bin got Fluffy's scent immediately. He stiffened in amazed excitement, then raced across the stable, emitting the hare's male call, which is like a wee foghorn, from the little sac under his chin. Fluffy shrank in terror. Bin stood by her and stamped imperiously on the ground with his big hind legs. He licked Fluffy's ears in eager admiration. Suddenly Fluffy understood. Her starting eyes softened and melted and closed. She turned and crept towards Bin and tucked her head humbly under his chest. Bin licked her ears more gently. Marion and I heaved a double sigh of relief and relaxed ourselves contentedly.

A very special romance was about to begin!

It sometimes crossed my mind that life for me was becoming very full – and that this in itself was surprising!

When I had agreed to give up my London studio and join forces with my family in their newly-found country home, it had seemed rather an onerous change to me. To settle down in a totally strange district where we knew nobody, and to live in almost complete isolation on four lonely acres, far from all one's town contacts and interests, had indeed been an undertaking. For no matter how much the possibilities of neighbourly friendships might develop, the fact remained that mine was a full-time job on the 'land', and that I took it seriously. Even Marion's company was enjoyed in short and sweet intervals, and so, I had thought, loneliness loomed ahead of me.

But I had reckoned without my book!

Day after day more letters streamed in – amazing letters, some from quite influential people, who encouraged me to go ahead in spreading my message and my propaganda for a new world. Soon, even parcels began to arrive, from Australia, from Canada – parcels of health foods, raisins, dates and nuts, all sorts of things no longer obtainable with our meagre rations – things, as they said, to keep my Muse alive! Marion looked on with amazement at these developments.

Later, even people began to arrive. They came 'to discuss ideas and seek advice'. Some of them were rather weird looking, shaggy-haired and unconventionally dressed.

Finally, the local police arrived to interview Marion.

Who were these people, seeking out our Grange? In times of war, and in our district, a sharp look-out had to be kept. What did these visitors want?

Marion looked at them helplessly.

'Well, you see – my cousin has written a book!'

The police knitted their brows.

'I see! Then we will have to interview your cousin!'

So I showed them my book and my letters.

After careful scrutinizing, they decided that there was nothing Communistic or Fascist – or any other 'ist' about my proceedings, and very doubtfully took their leave.

'Upon my word,' exclaimed Marion, 'having an authoress-relative is really something! One never knows what will happen next!'

And indeed I was soon kept so busy answering letters that it seemed like a job in itself. My readers wanted me to 'form a society' or send out newsletters, or write a study course, or, most terrifying of all, give lectures!

'And all this right in the middle of war!' I thought, as the thud of a not-so-distant land-mine reached my ears, and Bin came creeping hurriedly to take shelter beneath my chair.

It seemed obvious that more and more people were realizing the necessity for a different way of life – but *what* way? Whatever could I suggest?

This query had been at the back of my mind for many days. I began to long for the chance to ask Raphael about it. Of course I knew that I would have to write another book. But, meanwhile – what could I do about all those letters? All those wonderful eager people were anxious to progress, physically or mentally or in service to a new age! They constituted a challenge and a responsibility of which my untried and amateur enthusiasm was increasingly aware.

How could I, such a beginner in the ways of the spirit, meet the generous and understanding response which was flowing in? Evidently my little book had struck a note of hope and of enterprise which, in those black days of war, seemed like a straw to which to cling. The emphasis was on the whole world of wonder and of fulfilment which still existed in spite of and in the midst of all the growing horrors. It was a tiny counterblast to the vast war nightmare!

But how to go on? How to implement the hopes aroused?

I felt like a microbe, put in charge of growing an oak tree!

'But of course it is not *me!*' I at last managed to tell myself. 'Nothing that we do is ever our own, really – we are but channels for the Universal mind, channels for the Creator's Plan. I wrote my book through meditation, and in that same way I must continue. I am *not* a microbe! I am a cell of God's mind – Raphael has taught me that, and it is up to me – and to us all – to realize it!'

With these thoughts I braced myself to answer my letters with more confidence, and to devote myself more seriously to my daily meditation.

Night after night I watched the moon grow – for I had come to expect Raphael's arrival as soon as it was quite full.

More and more deeply, I pondered upon all that he had shown me so wonderfully. The fact of the underlying unity of all life was now clear to me. The processes of development, of interdependence, and of imbuement with inner lives were a constant source of inmost wonder, as I went about my work and tried to use my extended vision.

It was all marvellous, thrilling, and inexhaustible food for thought and imagination.

But did it answer my urgent need? Was it what I really yearned for?

I searched within myself. No, wonders and knowledge were not enough for me. I wanted more than anything else to understand *why* the world was in a mess – why man, with his marvellous brain and capacity for all that is noble, creative and lovable, could reduce himself to degeneration and violence far worse than any animal, and to an extent that threatened the very existence of his bountiful mother planet? I wanted to know *how* mankind could be awakened to realization and regeneration, so that a great reaction could take place and a new civilization could be built.

If my one amateur little book could bring me the response I was receiving, it meant that, could one but say the right word and suggest the right solution – with a pen of fire? – then one could *really* help.

Yes, that was what I desired – really to help our poor suffering, ignorant, stupid humanity (including, of course, myself) to learn to live a beautiful life in our beautiful world.

'Verity! Verity!' came suddenly the thrilling voice of Raphael. 'My faith in you is being justified. You are keeping to the main issue – you are getting down to fundamentals – what to do, and how to help – you have made me happy, my dear student!'

I gazed joyfully up at Raphael, suddenly standing at my cabin door.

'You are here! How wonderful!' I exclaimed. 'But I know that I desire the impossible! The world situation is too vast, too complex, too chaotic! Where would one begin?'

'Nothing is impossible! One with faith as a grain of mustard seed could move mountains! All right – you wish to move many mountains, in many spheres; well, your faith must be as strong *as many grains* of mustard seed – that is all!'

'Huh, that is all?' I echoed. 'Then I must acquire it. So, please, Raphael, show me the root of world trouble today!'

'We are coming to that by degrees, my dear,' said my friend, as he seated himself in the cabin. 'You must be patient and learn things in their right sequence. So we will return to outer space once more. Are you ready?'

'Oh, yes!' I said, and relaxed happily to await our next adventure.

8

Hidden Lives

It did not seem strange to me when for the second time I found myself floating rapidly upwards by Raphael's side, and soon leaving the Earth far behind me. I thought I knew what to expect. I imagined I had seen it all. So I quietly enjoyed the beautiful and mysterious scene. I gave a gasp of pleasure as the planets came into view, circling at their different speeds around the Sun.

Soon the solar system was seen in its entirety, clustered beneath our feet. I then realized that we had ceased our own rapid travelling and were poised in space, and commanding a full view of the brilliant Sun and his starry kingdom.

I watched intently, wondering if I would soon be able to discern the etheric web. Instead, however, I found that my eyes were focusing to view the giant astral bubble which encased the solar system. It was indescribably beautiful, with waves of iridescent colours passing softly through and around it. Surprisingly, the whole bubble was rotating as if upon an axis.

Quickly I turned to watch the bubble within which Raphael stood, erect and silent. There again I had an impression of rotation, of a very definite ordered circulatory motion.

'Quite right,' answered Raphael to my unspoken thought. 'I hoped you would observe it. You see, life is held within form through the activities of rotation. For instance, a solid metal or a stone is formed of atoms which are rotating upon their axes. You cannot always see the rotation but it is there, and causes one object to remain separated from another. And just as an atom is a miniature solar system so a solar system is really a large atom! Scientists have completed the first stage of smashing the atom. They know that there is powerful energy of life imprisoned within it. But they do not know that it is an individual life: a little living being which is using the atom as its body! That secret is still hidden from them. Therefore they use violence against the atom, and violence should never be used against any living being – it only creates Karma, or negative results.'

I pondered this carefully, whilst Raphael watched me intently.

'Then, if that is so with the atom,' I faltered at last 'and if the solar system is giant atom, then is a – a giant being imprisoned in the solar system also?'

'You have courage,' replied Raphael with obvious satisfaction, 'to face such a thought. You deserve to learn. Yes, my friend, that is indeed the case. The solar system is the physical body of a mighty Being, whose holy flesh it is impossible for us to see, but whose seven psychic centres (which in us are expressed physically through our principle endocrine glands) in Him are expressed through the seven major planets of His system. Now watch with the utmost reverence and I will guide your inner vision.'

So saying, Raphael moved towards me and gently placed his hands over my eyes.

'Continue to look,' he whispered, 'but do not expect to see that mighty Being – it is not permitted. What I will show is the way He has given birth to lesser lives for the purpose of running His Universe. Now watch!'

I gazed, and dimly, through the palms of Raphael's hands, I began to discern the solar system. I saw it as a huge living moving astral bubble and discovered that it was completely one – an entity. At its heart was the Sun which now looked like a hollow circle within the greater one. I concentrated upon the Sun and looked for the seven coloured strands of light, flowing from its planets. I saw them, but they looked different. They shimmered and pulsated like living serpents. With a shock I realized that I *was* looking at living beings – marvellous and glorious, vast lives, each of whom held one particular planet within his convolutions.

'What a marvellous sight,' I stammered, dazed by what I saw.

'Keep steady,' commanded Raphael sternly, his hands still firm upon my eyes. 'Now! turn and look at me!'

I slowly tore my eyes from that wonderful sight and turned them to face Raphael.

'But I can't see you, Raphael!' I cried in alarm, 'I can still see the solar system!'

'Nevertheless, my little one, it *is* at me that you are looking now. Continue looking and tell me what you make of it,' came Raphael's voice with the utmost gentleness.

I drew a deep breath, and tried to calm myself, as I gazed steadily in Raphael's direction. I blinked and looked again, but there before me still, was a small solar system around which I could dimly sense the outline of my friend's form. The central sun was at about the place where his heart would be. From it the seven coloured living strands swirled as serpent-like mermen, and at the core of each one was a fiery planet, every one of a different colouring.

'The sun is just at the place where your heart is,' I whispered eagerly. 'And higher up where your throat is I see a fiery planet, surely in the region of the thyroid gland! And higher up in the head another and yet another – and another below, where the solar plexus is . . .'

'Yes, you are beginning to put two and two together,' said Raphael suddenly. 'But don't spend all the time *looking*. Tell me to what conclusion you are coming!'

'But it is extraordinary,' I exclaimed at last, as revelation gradually dawned upon me. 'The solar system is in a way the glandular system of the Almighty – and each part of it is a separate life!'

'And we also are made like solar systems. Each part of our little solar system is a living being also – each of our centres or glands belongs to a separate living being within us – oh but that's impossible!' I broke off. 'Surely I am one being, not many?'

'Yes, you are one being, lord of your little universe; you are quite right. Yet you contain within your own life many lesser lives who run your system for you. Think! Do you make your own lungs breathe, your own digestion work? Then who does it? Someone, or ones, who know how – *you* do not know how! *You* know how to think, to move your hands, to deliberately focus your eyes! But you do not know how to manufacture compounds with endocrine glands! Your lesser lives – we call them "elementals" – *do* know!'

I silently turned my face from Raphael's direction and contemplated once again the great solar system below us. I was getting more accustomed to this new inner vision. I could already see that the vast luminous cluster below us was teeming with almost invisible living beings. The more I looked the more I saw: living, moving, busy beings great and small, semi-visible, as if each one were made of the stuff of a glittering soap bubble. The lesser beings were contained within the serpentine bodies of the greater beings.

'What are those seven great spirit-like beings into which the solar system has divided itself?' I gasped earnestly, struggling to understand what I saw.

'They are known by many names in many lands,'

answered Raphael. 'Have you heard of the Seven Spirits before the Throne? Or of the Seven Archangels? Have you heard of "all the Company of Heaven"?' Have you heard of the Cherubim and Seraphim, of the Forces of Light and the Forces of Darkness? Do all these terms mean something, or nothing at all?'

'Yes! Yes!' I answered hastily, 'I have often wondered. We are used to hearing those names, but they never seem actually *real* to us!'

'Why not?' came the abrupt retort. 'Is it easier for you to believe that all this Universe came into being, and continues to be run like clockwork, without any active intelligences at work behind it? The Being whose body we know as our solar system is He whom we call God. We have been taught that man is made in the image of God! Once again I ask you, does this mean anything definite or nothing at all? If God arranged that seven great lives containing many lesser lives, should run His Universe for Him, then we might expect that man, who is deity in miniature, is built upon a similar plan. And so it is! Life is so full of wonders that I can only teach you very little at a time, or you could not bear it! I will now give you the merest fleeting glimpse of the way in which many lives are a part of the greater life. Come! And do not forget what you will see!'

So saying, Raphael removed his hands gently from my eyes. He waited until I had established that my inner vision still remained with me.

Then he took my hand as we floated quietly down towards the solar system and entered within its aura.

The swirling rippling lives which had been clearly visible to me when I was looking at the Sun and his planets from a distance, became vaster and vaster to the eye as I approached. By the time that we were passing through the aura itself I was becoming confused by

what I saw. I still recognized that the many coloured
pulsations and ripples and waves around us were *alive*
but I could not imagine or see where they began or
ended.

'Raphael!' I called anxiously. 'How can something be
alive when it seems to have no form? The seven-coloured
forces or beings seem to be all mixed up now that we are
within them!'

'My little one,' replied Raphael, promptly moving to
my side, 'you are accustomed to think of forms and bodies
only in solid physical matter. That is very materialistic!
When you travel and "dream" in sleep, you slip out of
your "solid" body, and journey in your astral body which
is made of gaseous substance, but seems quite *real* to you
at the time. As regards the Seven Coloured Spirits, their
bodies are made of qualities and energies, and although
they never lose their individuality, they constantly inter-
mingle as they build the ideas that are expressed as the
physical world. If you take a large soap bubble and blow
into it seven puffs of smoke of seven different colours, they
would appear to mix completely and lose their individual-
ities. Yet if one were small enough to enter the bubble
the separate coloured atoms of smoke would be quite
distinguishable. Your eyes are unaccustomed to watching
the life at work within the form. Be patient! You will
see better in a little while.'

We were now approaching the Earth, as I could tell by
the way in which it was swelling rapidly below us. With
my new vision, however, even our familiar planet looked
different. I saw with amazement that deep below its
surface there appeared to be a glowing solar system much
like that which I had seen within the form of Raphael.
Very soon we were too near to the Earth for this impression to remain. But I did not forget it. I felt that Raphael
was now guiding me carefully, and selecting a vantage
point for that which he wished to show me. Finally we
came to a halt, poised at a distance above the Earth from

Eternal Fairyland

where land, forest, sea and mountain could plainly be distinguished.

'Now we are well within the Earth's aura,' he observed, 'and everything is more substantial here. It will be easier for you to see.' He approached me and placed his hands once again over my eyes.

'Now look!' he commanded.

I was very astonished. The whole scene was transformed so completely that I had great difficulty in grasping what it was that I saw, and would have found it almost impossible to describe. All the atmosphere was softly tinted like one continuous rainbow whose bands of colour rippled through and through each other, just like the ripples of water on a calm seashore. And, just as those ripples leave their shapes moulded upon the sand, so were those colours caught and held and reflected by the various objects upon the Earth: the green ray claimed the grass and the leaves as its own; the red ray tinged the red rocks and the poppies in the fields; the blue ray ruled the water and the sky.

I felt that the green which flowed through the atmosphere was indeed a great life full of meaning. As I gazed and gazed I was aware of a great green spirit-form brooding over the meadow which lay spread beneath us.

'That is a Deva!' announced Raphael. 'Each of the Seven Spirits contains many lesser lives to do the work, and they in their turn contain still smaller lives to do their bidding! Come closer, and you will see.'

As we descended rapidly to the surface of the earth, the great Deva's form was hardly distinguishable, but flowing down from his robes were many little green dancing figures, obviously very busy indeed.

'Fairies! Surely!' I burst out. 'But fairies are not *real?*' I interrupted myself in great puzzlement.

'And why *not?*' queried Raphael almost, it seemed, in exasperation. 'Fairies have been written about, described and painted, all over the world and throughout history, and yet people are so woodenly dull that they take it for granted that fairies do not exist! Of course they exist, in their millions and in every colour – nature could not carry on without them. They are helping everywhere all the time. Not a flower grows nor a fruit ripens nor a bird sings without the help of some of these lovely little beings. There are many ranks and degrees of them, and the tiniest are those who look after the atoms.'

By this time we were following the troops of fairies into the wood which fringed the meadow. Finally Raphael motioned me to sit with him beside a rippling stream.

'Now relax yourself,' he said gently, 'and learn how nature really lives.'

For a long time I watched silently, hardly believing what I saw. For the air was like a moving rainbow full of transparent coloured living beings of all shapes and sizes. They moved rapidly about their duties, guided apparently by unseen direction from their controlling Devas. They polished the long grass and seemed to pour green light into it. They hovered over the wild lilac like a faint mauve cloud. They passed through into the water and seemed to add to its froth and glitter. They were of so many shapes. I saw tiny goblins peeping from under the toadstools. I saw little water-sprites playing on the bank. I saw the birds coming to drink at the water's edge, and also a rabbit. It appeared that these birds and animals were all aware of the fairy creatures. In fact they often stopped to play with them. I saw the little sprites who were hovering about whilst caring for the flowers and the rabbits, pause sometimes to frisk and gamble around them, leaping sideways high into the air. The rabbits promptly imitated them. I suddenly understood the meaning of Bin's joyful pirouettes and coquettish shakings of the ears when apparently he was only in his own company.

'Some of these sprites have the work of teaching young

things how to play, an activity which is really most important to everyone!' whispered Raphael. 'Now watch that bird!' And he pointed to a large plump thrush perched on a bough above us in quiet contemplation.

As I watched, a beautiful orange-coloured fairy approached the thrush and began, apparently, to whisper in his ear. He cocked his head for a while to listen, then slowly stretched his little neck and let out a few introductory notes. The fairy chided and urged him and gradually worked him up until he was in full and glorious song.

'So Fairyland *is* real then,' I breathed to myself, quite enchanted by what I saw. 'I begin to understand now what it is that cats look at – and horses too.'

'Yes, and inebriated human beings,' smiled Raphael, 'who have partly freed themselves for a little while from the prison of habitual materialistic vision! Those rats and snakes which they see when "under the influence" are real creatures, of course, but not of a – shall we say – progressive type!' He paused and watched me intently.

'Are you contented with what you have learned today?' he asked me finally.

This startled me. I broke off from my rapt contemplation of the exquisite scene which was a glorified and vivified edition of Hans Christian Andersen and Arthur Rackham and Edmund Dulac all rolled into one, as I now felt. My thoughts also flew to Shakespeare and several of the poets, all of whom had treated the subject of fairies and goblins with the utmost seriousness.

'Evidently,' I began, thinking out loud, 'those men must have believed in them, and their descriptions and pictures tally, don't they?'

'They tally with ancient folklore and priestcraft all over the world,' replied Raphael, 'and directly an imaginative artist sits down to draw fairies, either he sees them consciously or subconsciously, or he links up with the vision of others who know them! But you haven't answered me – are you glad you have seen all this?'

I finally wrenched my mind free of its enthralling absorption and faced my teacher's question, raising myself up on my knees in the long grass the better to sum up what I saw.

'It is all amazing, wonderful, fascinating,' I began slowly, 'such beauty has to be seen to be believed, as well as the extraordinary activities which are going on around us to which we are completely blind! But,' I added as gradually my mind reverted to its normal surroundings, 'but, that is not what I asked you to teach me, Raphael. I want to know how ignorant, suffering humanity can be helped. I ache to know how disease can be avoided, how slums and horrible, ghastly wars can be prevented – and all you can do, after all your promises, is to show me – *fairies!*' I burst out in a rush of sudden, furious disappointment. 'Are you treating my longings with contempt, or is there indeed no answer to my question?'

My voice rang out in anger and as it echoed across the glade the scene changed like a flash. All the rainbow colours, the fairies and the sprites vanished as if they had never been.

'Dear! Dear!' exclaimed Raphael in concern. 'You have broken the delicate visual adjustment with all that violence. Now I can see the fairies and you cannot!' And he laughed almost teasingly.

I blinked and stared, but in truth I could no longer see anything unusual.

'I don't care!' I burst out, breaking, I am ashamed to say, into angry sobs. 'If I can't learn how to help people then I would rather not learn anything at all! If I am not going to see the reason for our existence then I don't want to see fairies! You had better show them to someone else.' Then I flung myself down on the grass and wept more despairingly than I had ever done before. For if Raphael could not help me, then who could?

Finally my sobs began to subside, especially as only complete silence came from Raphael's direction. In growing trepidation I peeped up through my fingers at my companion. I saw with a sudden shock that he was watching me with blazing eyes.

'How angry you must be!' I stammered brokenly. 'How rude I am and ungrateful! I know it! But I can't help it! You are quite fed up with me I suppose?' I dared not look at him.

'On the contrary!' came at last his unexpected reply in a voice which vibrated with vigour. 'I am extremely pleased with you. There are so many people, Verity, who crave knowledge merely from a sense of self-importance, or a wish to be thrilled or interested, or as a passing enthusiasm – or even for the love of knowledge itself! None of these motives is of any value. The only one which counts is love of God or of one's fellow men, which is the same thing. You have this love, Verity, and if you do not let yourself be led astray by wonders and delights, you will, I promise you, attain your heart's desire. But in order to help, one *must* understand – and you must learn what life really *is* and whither it is trending before you can help in the way you wish.'

My drooping spirits had revived at Raphael's earnest and kindly words.

'You mean,' I began wonderingly, 'that it is not really a waste of time to know about fairies?'

'The goal of all man's learning, the triumph of future science, will revolve round knowledge of that which you have been allowed to see today. The harnessing of atomic energy when it is finally done in a non-poisonous way, will depend on the use of these rainbow colours and of the notes that bird was learning. And, in that way only, will it be possible to overcome the disease and low standard of living which you rightfully deplore.'

I was astounded to hear these words. I looked searchingly into Raphael's brilliant eyes in my effort to believe him. From his steady gaze I seemed to draw a conviction of truth which was the strongest thing I had ever felt in my life.

'I believe you, Raphael!' I sighed at last. 'If you are not tired of helping me please show me some more.'

9

Beings Within Man

'So be it,' replied Raphael. 'I will now show you what part some of these little beings play in a human life. You may find it rather startling. We will have to shrink a little. Are you ready?'

'Yes,' I said. I stretched out my hand and gripped my friend's arm to reassure myself. It seemed a long time since I had done any shrinking.

Raphael broke into a merry chuckle.

'I notice that astral substance already seems quite solid to you!' he teased, 'I am glad you find such support from this gaseous arm of mine!'

I felt that we were about to move, and indeed we began to skim with great rapidity through the air. In about half a moment we came to a sudden halt. We were now in a long, white-walled room in which there were a number of people. Quite close to them a nurse was standing talking to a doctor. These two seemed to be discussing some of the people in the room whom, it was easy to see, were patients. Even at a distance the movements of the patients and the sounds of their conversation seemed slightly strange. With a shock I realized that we must be in some kind of mental hospital.

Raphael touched my elbow and spoke to me quietly.

'Yes,' he said, 'we are now in a lunatic asylum. But first of all we will study the sanest person in the room, who is the nurse. You will learn first how our lesser lives do their work when everything is normal. Now I will stimulate your inner vision, and we will reduce ourselves, but not very much. Are you ready?'

I nodded eagerly. The curious sensation of shrinking at once overtook me. The white room soon became a lofty hall full of looming distant figures, whilst the body of the nurse towered above us, and the crackling of her apron as she gesticulated to the doctor sounded very like noisy gunfire.

At this point Raphael turned to me and gently laid his hand over my eyelids. I knew what to expect, I thought, as I waited quietly, staring in the direction of the gigantic figure of the nurse. Gradually the whole beautiful and mysterious picture of life behind the form began to build up before my inner vision. At first I saw suspended above me the familiar solar system. Whilst I was busy trying to allocate the glowing planets to their positions near the heart, throat, brain and solar plexus within the towering form, I guessed that, had I not known I was regarding a human body, I would have felt convinced that only the heavens were before my view.

As my sight strengthened I saw the etheric web, which looked still more beautiful when seen on such a large scale. It reminded me more than ever of a great cobweb of neon lighting which took on the shape of a human form with all its organs. In fact it could easily be recognized as the framework upon which that form was built.

All this time my vision was growing clearer, which made the subtler substances of the life within the form ever more visible. From the brilliant sun which shone in the region of the heart the seven serpentine coloured rays could be seen streaming forth, their convolutions embracing the glowing planets within the various organs of the body. Their various colours gradually intermingled and weaved with a rotary movement until by the time they all reached the periphery of the body they had assumed the familiar look of the astral bubble. This could be seen encircling the great figure of the nurse to a considerable depth.

I gazed, fascinated, a score of questions on my lips.

Raphael arrested my busy mind with a touch of his magic fingers.

'No questions yet!' he whispered sternly, 'I want you to go on looking!'

Obediently I concentrated upon my wonderful new eyesight, and waited quietly.

'All that you are seeing now,' continued Raphael, 'would be visible to a really expert clairvoyant, although hardly any such people are sufficiently trained as yet. What I propose to show you next are the lives or intelligences which produce and run this body for their deity, the nurse. As she is a splendid and well-balanced person she makes a good subject for our study.'

As I watched and waited I began to see or to sense a great form which hovered within the aura of the nurse. It appeared to be made of auric substance, and it vibrated with life, with feeling, and with intelligence. It reminded me of the Deva spirit which I had seen brooding over the countryside. As I remembered all the little lives I had witnessed flowing out from his form to do their work, I recognized the same mysterious activity once more before me. Delicate beings of many sizes were streaming through this nurse's aura, each intent upon his work. These busy lives passed through each other without hindrance. The effect was of several cinematograph films superimposed one upon the other.

'You will find it very confusing at first,' warned Raphael, 'so do not strain yourself trying to see too much. Just concentrate on the things I will point out to you. Now come with me!'

So saying, he removed his hands from my eyes. I noted once again that my inner vision still remained with me. Together we floated upwards and entered the nurse's tremendous form, whose size was such that I knew we must be shrinking still more. The teeming life around us made me feel almost as if I were being buffeted by a rough but silent sea. On every side there was intense activity going on. Opposite to me was a beautiful spirit or fairy of a transparent orange hue. He was swaying back and forth with a careful rhythmic movement.

'That is the living creature, sometimes called an "elemental", who takes care of the stomach – one might say that the stomach is his physical body. He controls within himself many smaller lives who produce the various digestive juices and activate the lesser movements óf that complex organ, the stomach. Now let us look at the elemental who dwells in the heart and makes of it his body and his life's work.'

So saying, he drew me with him towards the region of the heart, and waited whilst I studied what I saw. It seemed that Raphael was continually stimulating and readjusting my sight so that gradually I could accustom myself to see more and more. It was as if I were learning to change the focus of my own eyesight, not as in ordinary life from distant to near objects, but from the physical to the etheric, from the etheric to the astral, and finally from the astral to the creative lives within it all. I began to realize that an involuntary clairvoyant could have glimpses of all that I now saw but without the guidance and help which I was receiving, without which these results would be confused and difficult to sort out.

As I approached the vast thundering heart of the nurse, I clung to Raphael's arm in some nervousness. As we stood, we were about the same height as this powerful organ, whose activity at that close range seemed so violent that I had to control a wish to recoil to a safer distance.

'Please remember that we are in astral form,' commanded Raphael, 'and that we could pass right through the heart undisturbed if we wished! Now, refocus your sight – and your hearing – from the physical to the etheric – and try to do it by yourself this time!'

I wondered what he meant by 'refocusing my hearing'. I took one final look at the amazing sight before me, at the tremendous pipes of various hues which connected up with the heart, at the intricate way in which it was suspended from the surrounding walls of the ribs, and at the alarming amount of movement both from the outer rib walls, the great network of living tissue at the sides, and the valves of the heart itself. The noise was also tremendous, something like machinery made of rubber might cause, thunderous and reverberating but not harsh or metallic: a succession of pumping, bubbling, sucking and creaking sounds, which made me feel quite dizzy.

Pulling myself together, I concentrated on trying to see the etheric double. It did not take me long before I felt quite definitely a reorientation of my consciousness taking place under my will.

Not only did the physical form of the heart begin to fade from my view as my etheric vision took its place, but I became deaf also to the physical noises. New and more delicate sounds were received by the more delicate counterpart of my ears. As the beautiful etheric heart came into view, I could faintly hear the slight hissing or humming sounds of the electrical life forces as they flowed rapidly along the various coloured 'neon wires' which formed a heart of cobweb, as it were, as the living basis of the physical heart. I noticed that the racing electric channels each hummed a different note according to its colour.

'How marvellous! How fascinating!' I murmured.

'Now focus for the astral plane,' commanded Raphael. 'We have a lot to get through today.'

Obediently I concentrated my mind on the astral counterpart and sure enough in a few moments I began to see it. Finally it broke through in all its glory upon my view. Indeed, the vision I had of the astral counterpart of that heart was too beautiful to describe. The coloured rays which poured serpent-like from its centre and swirled round it until they blended into its enveloping astral bubble, were of a luminosity, delicacy and splendour such as I had not before beheld. At their very heart I could just discern a golden ball of fire.

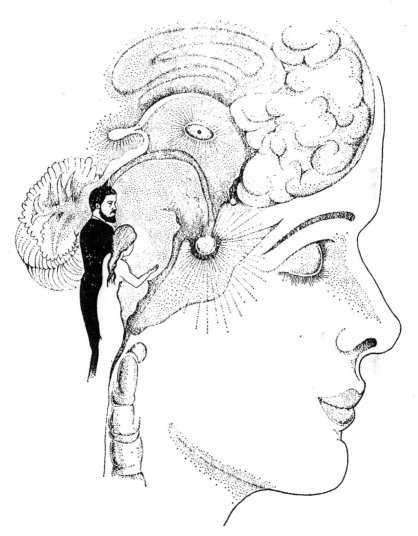

Mysteries within the brain

'Why – oh why – is it so much lovelier than anything else you have shown me, Raphael?' I whispered when at last I could find my voice.

'That is a question which concerns a great mystery,' came the grave reply. 'Our entire solar system has as its goal the expression of love. This planet will achieve that goal by means of human beings whose hearts are the instrument through which it will be transmitted. We do not yet know *what love is*. The love which humans and animals show is only the faintest beginning of the real thing. The heart of the solar system is the Sun, and the heart of the human being is also, in its inner essence, a little sun. Now look for the being who inhabits the heart and makes it work – the heart's "elemental".'

I once more tried to refocus my vision. Soon I began to see the form of the heart-spirit or Deva hovering or crouching within the sphere of the heart's astral bubble. He was very, very beautiful. His body seemed to be formed of warm golden light from which flowed a wonderful sense of peace, of comradeship and of understanding.

'The wisdom of the heart!' I thought as I gazed. The spirit or elemental did not appear to see us. He was sunk in deep concentration as he worked to produce the muscular and etheric activities within his body the heart. Various small beings could be seen under his control, working busily at the functioning of the different valves.

'Every organ in the body is run in the same way!' explained Raphael, following my observation with patient care. 'All the chemical compounds and juices, of which there are an infinite number, are compounded by little elementals, as clever or more clever than our modern chemists. The chemists have got as far as discovering and analysing these compounds in the blood (even copying them) but they still seem to think that they just "happen". They do not face the fact that complex happenings *must* have an intelligent initiator of some kind!'

'Yes, I quite see that,' I agreed thoughtfully, 'but supposing a man *did* know that all these elementals were working for him in his body – how would that help him?'

'That is a practical question!' smiled Raphael, well-pleased. 'In fact it is the crux of all that I am showing you. All these lives within a person's body are his servants, over whom he is intended to develop not only complete and wise control, but cooperation. If he but knew it, he is always able to communicate with them and express his wishes to them. If he is sufficiently single-minded they will understand and obey him. But their vices are a reflection of his own – be it laziness, lust for power, self-importance! If their lord and master allows any of them to become self-indulged the whole organization of his life becomes unbalanced. In a little while I will show you examples of this. But first I would like you to see the beings at work who help man's brain to function!'

So saying, Raphael glided rapidly away and I followed closely behind. I noticed that we passed swiftly upwards from the heart, through regions teeming with fascinating activities which I would have loved to explore.

Finally we came to a halt. I drew breath and looked around. We were evidently standing within the head of the nurse. There was a cave-like slope above us which was the roof of her mouth. This however, was only dimly perceptible because my senses were still functioning in the etheric vibrations. Therefore I saw the outlines of jaw and nose traced in the luminous webbing, but I could also see beyond, into the convolutions of the brain, which lay above us in its entirety.

'Now look up at the brain,' commanded Raphael, 'whilst I strengthen your sight still further!'

I began carefully to study the brain. It looked very like a large embryo curved upon itself, with some of its pro-tuberances taking the shape of budding limbs. Whilst I watched, I felt my eyesight refocusing. To my amazement the familiar sight of the solar system slowly dawned before me once again.

I blinked, I gazed, but there, sure enough, were the glowing fiery planets set like jewels in the neon webbing of the etheric brain.

I felt Raphael's gentle restraining hand as he quelled my growing excitement.

'Watch and study carefully,' he admonished. 'Remember this is *research* and not a pleasure trip!'

Abashed, I tried to get a grip on myself and watched the scene with an air of stoic calm that I was far from feeling.

I could see that the sun of this newly-found solar system was right in the middle of the head. Its most important neighbour seemed to be a luminous planet at the root of the nose. High above us, through the top of the skull, I could discern a most beautiful glowing fire-ball. Its many rays flowed out and curled over until it gave the effect of a great chrysanthemum made of living coloured light.

'Oh how glorious that is!' I sighed gazing upwards. 'It is more beautiful than anything I have seen yet.'

'You are looking at the channel through which spiritual life flows into the human being,' replied Raphael softly. 'In the East it is known as the Thousand Petalled Lotus. Each petal connects one with an aspect of cosmic life – but, my dear, you wrote about this yourself in your first book!'

'Yes Raphael, I know I did – but writing and theorizing is one thing, whereas *seeing* it for oneself is quite another thing, and that is just what I needed. I can see that marvellous Lotus revolving upon itself. In fact, all these centres seem to rotate – just as the great planets do,' I said as I watched. 'This one in the centre of the head has comparatively only a few petals – or are they rays? The one behind the eyes has fewer petals still. Surely that one is where the pituitary gland should be?'

'That's right. It is the centre of life behind the pituitary. Now watch!' commanded my companion.

I felt the usual subtle change of focus taking place within my vision. The scene before me showed forth an intensified life. I saw the aura of the pituitary planet. Within its bubble hovered a living luminous being, very intent upon its work. I could see that the pituitary was a very complex and important centre, from which ánd into which passed a constant flow of swirling coloured waves crowded with tiny little creatures.

'Do not look any more at this today,' said Raphael, pulling gently at my arm. 'There is so much to see here that it would bewilder you. The pituitary is like a kind of telephone exchange or bureau of information, where every experience and effort of thought is registered. The more abstract or idealistic thought produces strong radiations which reach out towards the central or pineal gland, that which is controlled by the little sun which you have seen. This latter is a transmitter from the uppermost centre, the Thousand Petalled Lotus. In a perfect human being these three centres or planets are firmly linked together, so that the personality (the pituitary) is influenced by spirit through the higher mind (the pineal), and all the elementals and living workers in the body can thus come under control. This nurse is a decent and balanced person, so everything here is working normally. Now I want to show you what happens when such is not the case. Let us move on, Verity!'

So saying, he took my hand. We passed with the extraordinary swiftness to which I had become accustomed, out of the great form of the nurse. We floated down the long length of the hospital ward and approached the looming figures of the patients. As we approached a strange feeling of nervousness and dread assailed me. I drew close to Raphael and instinctively sought protection within his aura. At once he turned to me and laid his arm kindly around my shoulders.

'I know how you are feeling!' he whispered. 'You will need courage for what I am about to show you. But please remember that nothing can hurt you unless you are afraid of it. Remember also that we are invisible.'

The horrors that I then witnessed were indelibly etched on my memory, although I would have preferred to forget them. In each of the patients of that hospital ward one or another of his elemental workers had swollen to abnormal proportions, and was conducting a reign of tyranny over the whole of the person's organism. In one case it was the elemental in control of thirst who had gained the upper hand. Instead of serving his lord and master he had been allowed to rule him. This elemental had become swollen and thickened and hideous, and had captured the whole attention of its owner, who only lived for his elemental's gratification, mostly in the form of alcohol. I could see that the other elementals at work within this patient's body were all demoralized and paralysed by the fumes of alcohol, and that the beautiful etheric web had many rents and gaps in it. Through these gaps floated astral forms of snakes, toads and rats. The patient evidently saw them for he shivered and shouted in terror.

'A case of delirium tremens,' explained Raphael. 'Those snakes and rats are the forms taken by certain low types of elementals who enjoy alcohol and are only able to function when they are near to it. If this patient were to pull himself together and conquer his craving for drink, it would mean that he had regained control of his drink elemental, who would gradually shrink back to his normal size and shape. Our elementals take on our human egotism, power-lusts and self-importance. They reflect us, their masters – and they can become our Frankenstein monsters.'

We next moved on to contemplate a patient who was sitting shivering with fear. From his brain a kind of astral cable linked him to a large dark grey ball of smoke which was packed within his astral bubble. Inside this ball of smoke I could see many activities going on – figures running, knives glistening, a kind of living nightmare. The poor patient seemed entirely engrossed and utterly terrified and was babbling to himself.

'That cloud is what we call a "thought-form" or an "obsession",' explained Raphael. 'It all began with self-pity which is a *most* dangerous activity and undermines the health very much. In this case one of the thought-elementals began to grow fat on this self-pity. He built himself up until now he rules his master from that little smoke-world of congealed thought he has made, so that now his master has developed persecution mania. If human beings knew of these elementals and exercised a balanced and disciplined *will*, these things would never happen, for the elementals are wonderful and willing *servants,* when controlled.'

I had become very absorbed:

'Then I suppose,' I began tentatively, 'that split personality, schizophrenia and other strange afflictions are all due to those elementals?'

'Not exactly to the elementals, but to the motive of their human master. They can be spoilt in exactly the same way as a dog or a child, and quickly learn to "take advantage". Otherwise they can be supremely faithful. Now tell me what you imagine is the matter with this next patient.' Raphael led me gently in front of a man who sat apart from the others as if sunk in a deep reverie.

I regarded him quietly, focusing and refocusing my eyes to see as much as I could. There was obviously something very wrong with this patient's astral bubble! It looked quite hollow and empty. I could see no beautiful colours swirling around within its circumference. In fact the bubble seemed to be coated with a thick grey smoke shell which prevented any rays from passing either in or out. Within this empty and cold shell its owner brooded, lonely and insulated from everything around him. Sometimes the other patients or nurses would approach him and even touch him, but they could obtain no magnetic response from him whatever.

I shivered. 'Is this a man who has made a fetish of loneliness?' I suggested, very puzzled. 'His face looks far too human for that!'

'You are right,' replied Raphael. 'He was a very loving individual. But he centred all his love upon one person – his wife – in a very possessive way and to the exclusion of everybody else. When his wife died she left a complete vacuum in his life which he preserved in selfish grief, until, as you see, it has become an impenetrable shell. He is suffering from what is called melancholia. Now look closer and see if you can discover what has happened to his beautiful coloured rays. He has prevented them from flowing outwards in the normal way towards all his fellow creatures.'

I approached the sullen figure and scrutinized his etheric web very carefully. I saw the planetary centres, dim though they were. I saw the beginning of the coloured rays as they sprouted from the centre, but they seemed at once to be arrested in their flow. They curled in upon themselves, forming tangled congested knots of force like short-circuited live wires. This smouldering coagulation was gradually burning and disrupting the body cells. The beautiful structures of both web and tissue were destroyed already over a large area.

'You are looking at a cancer!' said Raphael gravely. 'Brooding and resentment are very often the cause of a malignant growth. When you look at this man you can understand how it happens. It is always a case of misplaced energy so please consider that very carefully. That which we call *love* is really a radiation which flows to us and from us from the *Sun*. It should link us with all living creatures on the Earth in an exchange of understanding and co-operation. We human beings have made a travesty of the part we are meant to play in respect of that mighty Sun force. The result is disease, both mental and physical! Now watch!'

I looked round and saw that the nurse, whom we had already examined so intimately, was coming down the ward towards her patients, evidently to make sure that all was well. As she approached her aura could be seen radiating from the central sun of her heart soft golden rays which were indeed very like sunshine. She paused a moment and stretched out her hand to touch a bowl of flowers appreciatively with her fingertips. To my amazement I saw a vivid response awaken in the blossoms, but this response came from their quivering etheric counterparts which seemed literally to drink up those golden rays with a passionate thirst.

'*Love feeds!*' remarked Raphael briefly. 'Ignorant folk would say she had "green fingers" and not trouble to wonder what that really meant!'

The nurse was now talking to the patients, the healing rays from her heart and her fingers linking her up with them so that her mind could travel down their length and literally dwell within her patients' brains with complete understanding. Whilst she was there the obsessions and the fog clouds melted and wavered, but when she left them the old conditions re-asserted themselves once more.

'She is a fine person and loves enough to heal, but not lastingly,' explained Raphael. 'For a real cure *knowledge* is needed as well as love, the sort of knowledge that I have given you today, which would enable the patients to be taught how to heal themselves. So now, Verity, you are at last beginning to learn what lies at the back of disease. Now I think you have enough to ponder about until next full moon. So we will finish our adventure for today.'

I looked up gratefully at my wonderful friend.

'Oh I can't bear not to see you for a whole month!' I cried suddenly and impulsively.

'My dear student,' responded Raphael gently, as his shining eyes rested thoughtfully upon me, 'you have much work to do on all that I have taught you today. You must study this knowledge in your heart, make it your own, find out what it has done for you. By next month you must be able to tell me what you want next to learn. Now, home you go, and may you learn joy through today's experience!'

10

At the Earth's Core

'It will soon be midsummer,' I thought as I hurried out to my work one glorious sunny morning. 'The days go by so swiftly and there is so much to do that I hardly have time to think!'

I paused at the stable door and looked over the top to see if Fluffy needed feeding. I did not expect to see the Angora, because Fluffy suffered from persecution mania, and always rushed into the corner when anyone approached. She seemed quite as dumb as all of her kind were reputed to be. On this occasion, however, to my surprise, Fluffy rushed up to me effusively and sat with bulging eyes and stiff ears with quivering tassels atop, the picture of tense excitement. In her mouth was a stiff wisp of straw, which stuck out on each side like large artificial whiskers and made her look quite ridiculous. She anxiously approached me, her shyness forgotten through her intense urgency.

I stood still, nonplussed, gazing at her. Suddenly illumination dawned.

'Oh you poor darling!' I exclaimed, 'I believe you have just realized that you are going to have a family and you want to build a nest! Of course your hutch is too small! Wait a moment, I know just the thing!'

I excavated Bin's enormous disused hutch from amongst a pile of packing cases and set it down in a corner of the stable. It was full of straw. Fluffy bounced into it without a moment's hesitation. She took possession of it with much housewifely fuss and tidying up. Bin, hearing all these noises, was scratching indignantly at the stable door, wanting to join his wife.

'No Bin! I'm afraid Fluffy would not welcome you today,' I said. 'She has other ideas. I think I had better put you with the hens, if they don't object to you, now that they have chicks. Come along and we'll find out!'

The hen-run made a pleasant picture. The grey speckled mother was proudly pacing the grass, followed by her dainty little chicks, who ran to her obediently when she clucked, to follow her suggestions about diet. She was not a very energetic hen, but occasionally she would condescend to dig them up a worm or two and then there was great excitement.

Into this domestic scene Bin entered, unconcerned and still thinking about his wife. If she could have a nest, so should he! But, being a hare, he wished to make, not a rabbit hole, but a nice hollow saucer of earth in which he could lie full-length. He lolloped up to the apple tree and, selecting his spot, began digging furiously. His trim little front paws worked like lightning, scratching away the earth, whilst his heavy back legs scooped the loosened soil and flung it behind him.

Up rushed the baby chicks to watch this sudden activity. Here, surely, was a new kind of hen, much better at digging up worms than their own mother! They crowded round Bin, dodging his flailing feet, trying frantically to reach the dislodged worms.

Mother hen clucked at them authoritatively but she was quite outclassed. Bin stuck his whiskers out once or twice to find out what all these little yellow balls were tickling him for. Then, his nest completed, he heaved a great sigh and flung himself down in it with delight. The chicks were frantic. What sort of behaviour was this? To uncover some lovely grubs for them and then lie down on top of them? They dug and poked under Bin's fur trying to get at their hidden feast. Bin liked this attention, he chewed happily and then closed his eyes, whilst poor mother hen continued to circle her prodigal children and cluck to them in vain.

I pulled myself together. This would never do. There were about 100 lbs of gooseberries waiting to be picked, up in the walled garden. The rest of the village had picked their gooseberries long ago. They believed in eating their first gooseberries at Whitsun, at which time they were usually unripe, hard and small. This seemed to me to be both unhealthy and extravagant, but it was the custom of the district – whereas if you left your gooseberries they became quite luscious fruit as the weeks passed! In fact, in the wild orchard, where the birds could not get at the fruit because the bushes were engulfed in nettles and brambles, you could be sure of picking sweet blackcurrants as big as cherries, and gooseberries the size of plums long after their season was over. Even some of the forgotten strawberry plants in the long grass produced prize fruit at times. As I thrust my fingers carefully through the prickly gooseberry bushes I wondered whether all the weeding and digging and pruning were really the ideal procedures.

Of course one obtained big 'prize' vegetables and fruit thereby, but they were somewhat tasteless. The advantages seemed to be offset by an appalling amount of blight and grubs and disease affecting both tree and plant everywhere. Here indeed was a problem that I would very much like to put to my astonishing secret friend. Yet what was it exactly that I should ask him?

Once again I found myself faced with the simple problem of the soil itself. I had grown used to it. I was intimate with it in the firm, unthinking manner of a nurse with her child. I combed it and brushed it and fed it, so to speak, and I obtained the growth and response from it which I expected. Indeed, like all my fellow toilers, I took the soil for granted without having the faintest idea what it actually was.

In a sudden access of curiosity I relinquished my gooseberry picking and flung myself down close to the soil. I caught up a handful and crumbled it through my fingers. I laid my face down on the granulated surface and squinted earnestly at the tiny particles. A worm recoiled hastily from my alarming presence and anxiously worked his way into the loose earth. He was soft, fleshy, defenceless and wet – utterly different from the substance on which he apparently thrived, and not only the worm but all the delicate plants, the great ancient trees, the animals and insects and human beings themselves – all obtained their nourishment and their infinite diversity from the same uncompromising-looking substance which returned me stare for stare without giving away any of its secrets.

Raphael had hinted to me that our planet was alive – a living creature with a consciousness and a destiny to accomplish: with fiery centres of life and with unknown interior organs analogous to my own. Was I, then, walking about upon the epidermis of this great Being, and did He feel me? And what did it mean to Him if plants grew and if the grass was green? Could I know more about this amazing subject, and what would it avail me if I did?

My heart gave a great bound as this question finally formed in my mind. I turned suddenly as if conscious of a presence behind me, and beheld Raphael standing calmly watching me from the garden path.

It was the first time I had seen him in daylight. How fine-looking he was, this friend of mine! He seemed to radiate a kind of healthful glow in the same way as all the flowers and plants in the garden were doing. How different he looked from the farmers and gardeners, bent and dingy in their sombre-coloured clothes: or from the country women with their ugly shoes and stockings, their weatherbeaten faces, their ungainly movements, and their peculiar speech. Raphael was unhurried, gracious, vibrant: he brought an added beauty and an added interest to the scene, for reasons which I had not yet discovered.

'When you've quite finished summing me up,' smiled the new arrival, 'we can begin today's study!'

I felt myself blushing, and scrambled to my feet.

'I *am* glad to see you!' I exclaimed warmly. 'I suppose I do not need to tell you what I want to know!'

'You are anxious to get an understanding of the soil itself, its relation to the planet and its relation to you. Is that not so? Well, we will have to do some rather drastic exploring to make all that clear. In fact we will have to begin by penetrating to the very bowels of the Earth – and I mean just that! Does the idea alarm you?'

'Yes,' I said promptly, 'but I know it will be worth it! Everything you show me seems to be building up into an astonishing kind of giant Plan, and I feel that I may suddenly get the key to the whole of it.'

'The Plan!' echoed Raphael, with obvious pleasure. 'I have been waiting to hear that word from you. Keep it in mind – it will unlock many mysteries for you. Now are you ready? We will sit down on this bench and leave our bodies here.' He immediately seated himself and leant back as if he were going to slip into a doze. I followed suit, but a sudden thought struck me.

'Supposing someone comes into the garden while we are – asleep?' I asked anxiously.

'If your body is disturbed it will wake up, as we call it!' explained my companion. 'In other words, it will send a message along your life-line and you will return to it instantly.'

'Yes, but what about you?' I queried, still a little worried. 'Supposing someone came here and found me sitting silently with a perfectly unknown gentleman? That might rather spoil things!'

'You need not worry!' said Raphael quietly. 'That will not happen!'

I was about to continue my questioning when a familiar whirring feeling interrupted me: I was in the act of leaving my body almost automatically, and I knew a great pride. Sure enough, the process was rapidly completed and I found myself standing beside Raphael, gazing down at my sleeping form on the bench. But my companion pulled me away rather brusquely. I had a momentary feeling that he was trying to hide something from my view. I glanced quickly round the garden, which looked entrancing seen thus with my subtler vision. All the plants and trees quivered and gleamed with a radiant filmy lustre, each living form radiating its colourful emanations just as if, I thought, its very perfume were visible. But my chief surprise came when I glanced at the soil itself. For it, too, was radiating: a pulsating film of coloured life seemed to be beating outwards from it, from the facets of its thousands of different molecules. A butterfly settled suddenly in the sun at my feet. I saw that its aura, which was more beautiful than the insect itself, rayed outwards in a large circle all around it.

'Come!' said Raphael. 'You can look at all that afterwards. I want to show you our Mother Earth, from the core outwards. Now follow me!'

So saying, he swayed forwards suddenly and dived straight downwards through the gooseberry bushes and disappeared.

I gasped. Of course I remembered that I was in my astral form, but still! Gooseberry bushes! He really might have chosen another spot for his dive!

A suspicion that he was teasing me nettled me so much that I forgot the gooseberry prickles and dived with all my might. As I had expected, there was no solid obstruction to my passage and I shot downwards into the Earth at a tremendous speed. As soon as I could slow myself up I came to a halt and looked around for Raphael, only to discover that I had left him far behind and that he was sailing majestically towards me. When he came near me I could see that there was a twinkle in his eye.

'I didn't ask you to behave like a rocket!' he commented

drily. 'Please remember that you do not have to use any driving force when out of your body – or you might go out of your mind as well! Now *there* is something for you to think about, whilst we make our long journey to the centre of the Earth!'

The idea of being able to leave one's mind as well as one's body was certainly arresting, and it diverted my attention from my surroundings as we speed down wards.

Perhaps that is what it was meant to do. Soon we approached an enormous sun, and our speed gradually abated. This sun was vast and glowing. It seemed to be belching out flaming radiations at regular intervals, like the beat of a giant heart.

'You are right,' whispered my thought-reading friend. 'This is the heart of the Earth!'

As I gazed I thought I could see or sense a great form hovering over, or embracing, the sun in much the same way as the heart elemental who had crouched over the heart of the nurse.

I felt rather overcome. I shrank up against the side of Raphael.

'I don't know whether I can *bear* to see all this!' I faltered in trembling dismay. 'Its all so – stupendous – so unexpected – it is too much for me!' And I bowed my head in an access of something that felt like shyness.

My companion took me quietly by the shoulders and turned me towards him. I continued to hang my head obstinately, until I realized that nothing at all was happening. Inevitably this caused me to peep up in curiosity at Raphael. With a shock I saw that two large glittering teardrops were hanging in his eyes and that he was not looking at me at all.

'Raphael!' I whispered urgently. 'Raphael! What's the matter?'

He gave a start, tossed away the teardrops and turned to me with a faint smile.

'Ah, my dear,' he said, shaking his head at me, 'you remind me of the days long long ago when I set forth on the same search as you now make. But you are more lucky than I was. I was alone! And I saw many horrors, because I had no guide to protect my vision like you have! And yet your courage deserts you! I am sorry that I am of so little help to you.'

I rallied fiercely at this suggestion.

'I'm an ungrateful coward!' I cried vigorously. 'Show me the worst things you can, and so long as I have you, I will be all right!'

'I'm glad you've said that,' responded my friend quietly, 'because as a matter of fact there *are* rather fearsome beings at work under the crust of the Earth. But I am not going to show you very much – only a few glimpses to give you a general idea. So do not ask me any questions – just quietly memorize what you see.'

We were circling slowly in front of the great Sun whilst Raphael said this. I composed myself to observe everything intently. So well did I manage this that I forgot myself entirely. Therefore any sense of personal fear, which I otherwise might have experienced, was not able to capture me.

We were drawing further and further away from the central Sun as we circled. We passed outwards through successive spheres, each containing different substances and activities and which were enclosing the central core like layers of an onion. The incandescent Sun was peopled, as I now observed, by many beings great and small of curious shapes which reminded me of mythical creatures of folklore and fairytale. Serpent forms were there, and dragons, and tiny little leaping creatures like lizards – all with bodies which seemed made of fire.

'The smallest ones are the salamanders!' whispered Raphael. 'They could also be seen dancing in your own fire place had you a keen enough vision. No, don't speak! We are now moving outwards into the next sphere. We are now in one of the mental regions of our planet. Look around!'

The circumference of the Sun centre grew smaller as we receded from it. We were now moving round in a large belt of blue atmosphere which was also peopled with many busy forms and shapes of familiar objects.

'The fiery Sun you have been watching is really an evenlope or belt of fire which encloses the inner spheres of the Earth, which we are not permitted to behold, – the secret places of the mind and heart of the Earth's spirit. The stratum where we are now contains the invisible "seed-thoughts" of everything existing on the Earth. These thoughts take more concrete form as they pass outwards through the next stratum, the water stratum.'

'See! We have reached it ourselves, and you can observe that the shapes here are more solid. From here we will pass outwards to the sphere of vapour, and there you will notice that the forms are becoming imbued with life and with the urge to *be* and to grow.'

'Now we are approaching the stratum immediately under the Earth's crust. This, as you will notice, is half way between liquid and solid. Substances here are explosive and of a jelly-like quality, such as is lava. There is also oil – much oil, as you know. On the outer layer or stratum, the Earth's crust, we will find the layers of rock. These correspond to the strong bony skeleton, with a very thin *skin* of fertile soil on the surface. One might say that the Earth is a being who keeps his bones near his skin, his oily and flesh-like substances further inside, his bodily heat still further within and his brain and heart at the core of it all. Now that our journey is nearly over, if you have any questions, Verity, you may ask them. Let us rest here awhile.'

So saying, Raphael drew me to a ledge of rock which fringed the sea of lava-like substance churning around us. We sank down upon the strange support and my teacher waited patiently for me to speak.

'There was so much to see,' I exclaimed, as I tried to sort out my impressions, 'and everything reminded me of things you have already shown me. I saw the coloured astral life everywhere. I saw the same human thought forms, some good, some bad. I saw goblins and Devas and animal forms – in fact I should say that there are replicas within the Earth of everything taking place upon its surface. Why should that be?'

'In your own mind,' responded Raphael earnestly, 'there is a replica, as you call it, of everything taking place all over your body.'

'Yes – but *where* is the mind of the planet. How does it work?'

'There!' exclaimed my companion, almost gleefully. 'That is the question I have been waiting for! How does *your* mind work, Verity?'

I frowned and thought earnestly.

'I understand,' I began slowly, 'that the brain is not the *mind* but is merely its kind of receiving station. I realize that the mind is like a kind of body which is diffused all over the physical form.'

'You are right!' agreed Raphael, 'But a body must be made of cells – in this case, of living cells of what we loosely term electricity, or of a finer substance than astral substance. Each of our mind cells is a microscopic mind all on its own, just as each of our blood cells contains the complete history of our body. Well, where does that lead us? Where, then, are the mind cells of the planet – which we must expect to find all over his body?'

'Oh Raphael, that's too difficult – I can't guess!'

'Who – or what – are *thinking* all over the planet?'

'I don't know of any thinkers except people,' I admitted almost sulkily.

'Well – and why not *people*?' came the answer very quietly.

I looked up into Raphael's eyes earnestly, gropingly, desperately.

'Do you mean' I stammered, 'that human beings are –
or express – the planet's mind? – that the single human
mind is a planetary mind cell?'

'Exactly!' said my companion with obvious satisfaction.
'The planet depends for its progress upon the progress of
human beings. Their motives influence the planet's astral
body and emotions. The evil thought forms, greeds and
passions of men accumulate within the inner strata you
have seen, poisoning the life of the planet until waves of
emotional unrest are set up. A feverish condition ensues.
The accumulated poisons are cast off as in the human
being, through planetary sicknesses. These take the form
of tempests, droughts, pestilences, earthquakes, and vol-
canic eruptions! A volcano, after all, is but a planetary
carbuncle!'

'What then do man's *good* deeds and thoughts do to the
planet?' I asked, enthralled.

'Ah! *they* help to bring about the Plan behind it all –
they speed up progress! Man seems like a mere microbe
upon the Earth's surface until you realize his function as
the mind-in-action of the Earth itself. Then his immense
importance becomes apparent. Without him this planet
would be impotent – static! Upon him all the other four
kingdoms depend for their intercommunication and progress.'

'Which four kingdoms?' I asked.

'First the mineral kingdom, then the vegetable kingdom,
then the animal kingdom, and finally the spiritual kingdom. Mankind's struggles and activities bring to each of
these kingdoms contact with *mind* and thus stimulation to
progress. We all have an immense responsibility and task
in respect of all these kingdoms! Come, we can move now.
We will pass through the crust of the Earth and you must
watch carefully.'

So saying, Raphael took my hand and we floated gently
upwards. We passed through layer after layer of rocky
formation, passed underground lakes and caverns, through

various seams of flint, coal, chalk, clay and marble. I watched anxiously for a final outer layer of soil to appear. I wanted to see how deep it was.

Raphael paused.

'Before we get back to our soil,' he said, 'I want you to have a look at the radiations which are at work around you. I will strengthen your sight so that you can see them!'

I looked carefully in all directions. My subtilized vision allowed me to trace our route back towards the centre of the Earth in one direction and forwards to the Earth's surface in the other direction. From both quarters I could see the lines of energy or rays. The radiations from the inner Sun of the Earth pulled strongly, and I began to pay attention to them. The rays which came from the outer Sun of the solar system also pulled. There were many other rays too, pulling in all directions. I began to feel as if I were in the middle of an intricate spider's webbing made of rays, each of differing magnetic quality.

'These rays play through all life all the time of course!' explained Raphael. 'But I am stimulating your sensitivity to them today. Now we will pass upwards through the Earth and you will observe what happens where all these rays meet.'

We were now moving very slowly upwards through a complicated series of different strata of rock of various kinds. I recognized more seams, probably of coal and other ores.

'I see something glittering over there,' I cried suddenly, 'is it a diamond?'

'Yes,' answered my companion, 'it is a diamond. But you are seeing the etheric inner fire of the diamond. Its physical structure would appear dull because it has not yet been found and cut and polished, but its inner fire, as you observe, is most beautiful, and it will serve our present purpose. Look closely into it and see if you can discover any of the rays passing through it.'

I was very intrigued. I bent low over the diamond and gazed at it patiently, until my eyes adjusted themselves to its subtleties. Seen thus with its etheric double, the stone was indeed exquisite. The delicate neon webbing outlined, of course, the inner structure, the skeleton, as it were, of the jewel, which by reason of its transparency is not usually seen. This inner structure looked like a study in geometry, a series of intersecting triangles. Down each of the living wires which duplicated these formations, the living, pulsating fires of life could be seen racing, just as I had seen them in my own body. From where did that living electricity come?

I gazed enquiringly into the atmosphere surrounding the jewel. I could still see the numberless rays playing through the Earth from all directions. Some of them met and intersected within the diamond and their points of intersection coincided with the structural triangles which formed the jewel. As the rays passed into the gem they seemed to *become,* as it were, both the neon webbing and the life racing through it.

'I am *trying* to understand!' I whispered earnestly as I watched. 'Is it the rays which bring the stone into being?'

'Some of the rays are positive, some are negative, so-called,' answered Raphael, 'When two such meet anywhere in life, a pole, or polarity is set up, and a form crystallizes around it. All the rays come from the Sun or planets of our own or other systems. Each ray has different qualities and chemical potentialities. Where they intersect, compounds of all substance and form are built. Now let us move on further. Watch the rays please!'

So saying, he drew me away from my absorbed contemplation of the diamond. We passed very slowly upwards, until some new and strange-looking objects came into view. These were long, curving, branched white fronds, stretching downwards, fringed with delicate hairs and glowing with blue phosphorescent light.

I felt very astonished.

'Don't you recognize them?' laughed my friend. 'Those are roots – the roots of a great tree.'

As we both continued our ascent I at last beheld the soil. I saw for the first time how little of it there really is. Compared with the vast organism of the Earth planet, its thin layer of fertile soil was comparative in thickness to the skin of a human being. As I watched the great branching roots of the tree converging upwards towards the base of the trunk, I noticed countless movements of life all around it. Tiny creatures, worms, grubs, minute insects and microscopic bacteria – all were visible to me by reason of the phosphorescent glow of their etheric counterparts. My surroundings were teeming with life. I could see that all these creatures, great and small, were dependent for their existence upon the roots of the tree and upon each other. A constant interchange of metabolic processes was taking place.

The larger of these creatures lived by eating the roots or sucking the sap. Upon the by-products of their existence the smaller creatures lived. The tiniest bacteria were busy feasting upon the life processes of their larger neighbours, and producing compounds in the soil which the roots of the tree were able to absorb. It was a cycle of mutual assistance, each type of creature being dependent upon the existence of all the other little lives. I could see all this very plainly, because the constant stream of life which was passing from one type of creature to another was clearly visible through the pulsating etheric channels which outlined it all. Furthermore, now that I had been taught to notice the Cosmic, Earth and Sun rays, I could still see them playing from all directions upon this scene of busy activity, and pouring their vitality through it all.

Just here, at the depth – where the tree roots were thickest, was the place where the inner and the outer rays converged, met and intersected. There was a terrific sensation of pressure and of pull which made me sway where I stood.

'At this point,' explained Raphael, reading my thoughts, 'the Earth's gravitation (or magnetism) reaches its maximum strength. If it were not so, the crust of the Earth would fly off into space with a vast explosion, and all would be disintegrated. The pull from the Earth's core draws the roots downwards and makes them grow downwards. The pull from the Sun's gravitation or magnetism draws the plants out of the Earth and makes them grow upwards. The pull from the Moon's magnetism causes horizontal growth of plants and movements of tides of all kinds. The rays from all the other planets cause crystallization into the different shapes. Certain shaped atoms crystallize into different molecules, and these form larger crystals in accordance with their kind. Everything is built upon crystal formation, which itself is produced through intersecting lines of force or rays from stellar bodies, some of them vast distances from our solar system.'

'How marvellous it all is,' I breathed, quite overcome by what I was beginning to understand. 'Then, actually, the rays from all these stellar bodies do influence and produce life and living conditions on Earth? But surely that is what Astrology teaches?'

Raphael smiled.

'Of course it is!' he agreed, 'but then, Astrology is the greatest of all sciences – in fact it is the father of all sciences. Remember though, that I am not talking about *astrologers!*' he continued with a merry twinkle. 'They are mostly as fallible as are our economists, agriculturalists and other so-called "specialists". It takes incompetence in all walks of life to produce a world such as we have at present!'

I looked at him silently, thinking over the implications of this remark as we still continued on our way.

'But why so much incompetence, in spite of all humanity's brilliant scientific achievements?' I asked finally.

'Because,' came the reply, 'people rely on their *present* brain and intellect, and ignore the wisdom and experience of the past. They do not yet know that mystery, sacredness and spiritual laws are all scientific facts! Now, think about that, Verity!'

The Answer to it All?

Our wonderful journey was drawing to an end. Our earthy surroundings took on a more and more familiar aspect.

Presently I noticed that we were passing through a patch of soil which seemed quite devoid of living organisms. The healthful etheric channels were almost obliterated, the busy worms, insects and bacteria had all shunned it. The only remaining life seemed slimy, gangrenous, and evil. Downwards through this unhappy patch of soil some dead roots stretched in stark lifelessness.

'Why is this patch of soil so diseased?' I asked.

'Ah, now you can see what some of those artificial fertilizers have done!' exclaimed Raphael. 'Those roots belong to a pear tree – one of yours! Your predecessor in this garden wanted to force its growth. He applied a patent fertilizer which acted like a drug or alcohol does on a human being. There was false stimulation at first, a super-crop of rather tasteless fruit. Then the crude overdose of chemicals which could not be assimilated, settled into the earth and became a poison! The tree is dying!'

'But surely people know better by now than to poison their plants?'

'People know better than to poison themselves, but they still do it!' retorted Raphael. 'Humanity has been deliberately killing itself off, all through history!'

'How?' I queried, rather anxiously.

'Why, by taking poison into the mouth of course! Practically everyone commits suicide that way – by which I mean they shorten their lives by far more than half. Man's average expectation of life today is 60 years, whereas it ought to be about 200 years!'

'What do you mean, Raphael!' I cried, exasperated. 'Are you suggesting that I could live to be 200 years old?'

'*Why not?*' rapped out Raphael with an almost angry emphasis.

This time, however, he found himself faced by me in a real fury. I could hardly find words adequate to my feelings.

'How *can* you talk like that,' I stormed at last, 'when you know that I trust you and try to believe all you say? How do you expect me to take you seriously any more!'

'I do not expect a person suffering from poisoning to respond correctly to any practical remark,' retorted Raphael quite mildly. 'On the whole you manage remarkably well!'

'Do you mean to say that *I* am poisoned?'

'Certainly you are! You eat the same as everyone else, don't you? With some people the poisons take longer to act than others – that is all!'

'Raphael, *please!* please,' I broke in almost ready to weep, 'do explain what you are talking about!'

'That is easy! You only have to read the opening chapters of the Bible to get at the simple truth. There we are told that God created the fruit of the trees and the seeds to be man's food, and the green herbs to be the food of the animals. The human dental formation is the same as the gorilla's and the ape's, and they are fruitarians. Anyway, there is the simple fact stated in Genesis. Man has ignored it by turning cannibal and preying upon the animals – his younger brothers and his sacred charge. Such sacrilege has upset all his natural reactions and all his appetites have thereby become abnormal. He has become so diseased that he cannot think clearly about anything. Even the fact that in Southern Russia there are many peasants who retain youth through a very spare

vegetarian diet, so that one of them has become Lord
Mayor of his little town at the age of 150 years – even
these well-known facts do not awaken people to any clear
thinking.'

'What would the difference be if we were all fruitarian?'
I asked with deep interest.

'Fruit contains no poison. All other food does. Fruit
cleanses and renews the body, which need never grow
decrepit on a diet of fruit – Nature's true food for man.'

'But – but – doesn't anyone know of this, if it is really
so?'

'Throughout history there have been people who have
known and who have lived to a great age in splendid
health. Many such demonstrations have been made to
humanity. But none are so blind as those who will not
see. Humanity is a slave to its pork and beans and dough-
nuts and beer! In order to obtain all its unnatural desires
it upsets the balance of nature everywhere, produces soil
erosion and disease: and ceaselessly chops down those very
trees which were created to supply its needs.'

'But, surely,' I argued, 'if we all lived off the trees there
would be even more food shortage than there is now?'

'On the contrary,' declared Raphael, 'fruit and nuts
are so sustaining, so purifying both mentally and physically, that many things would happen. People would lose
all their unnatural appetites. Their new diet would prove
to be so satisfying that they would eat far, far less. As more
and more trees were planted, rainfall and climate would
improve, deserts would disappear: animal life, left to itself, would adjust itself. Animals, no longer preyed upon
by men, would cease to be dangerous, even cease to prey
upon each other. From trees and shrubs man can obtain
all his needs, wood for building, cotton, paper, cork, rubber, medicine, clothing, and all the food he requires.
Living thus, man would lose his stupidity, cruelty and
acquisitiveness; war and disease would cease for ever.'

'So is *that* the answer to it all?' I asked wonderingly.

'Would a fruitarian diet be the means of salvaging human-ity?'

'That is not the complete story,' replied my teacher calmly. 'For instance, we know that Hitler is a vegetarian but that does not help the world. No, the first require-ment is for mankind to get a reaction from its present mode of living, and to decide at last to try to be really honest spiritually. That means facing a few simple com-mandments: "Thou shalt not kill" for instance! That means no wars and no meat! and no furs or leather, and no animal serums. Then again: "Thou shalt love thy neighbour as thyself": that means no exploitation of ani-mal, plant, soil, water, and of one's fellow men; no profiteering, no usury, no slums, even perhaps no miners!'

I did not reply. I was thinking deeply, so deeply that I hardly noticed that we had passed upwards into the sun-shine and were back in the walled garden once more. I was brought to myself by hearing the familiar little snuf-fling noise that Bin always made when he wanted to attract my attention. I realized that Raphael and I were sitting once more on the bench and that Bin was at our feet, raised up on his haunches in an attitude of patience and expectancy.

'Your intelligent little friend has been trying to wake you,' said Raphael, smiling tenderly. 'He knows it is tea-time! Now before you lose your etheric eyesight, look at him carefully and tell me what you see!'

I gazed intently at the sleek little white figure before me. I could see his etheric double, the most perfect one I had so far examined except Raphael's. I could also dis-cern his beautiful astral bubble which pulsated with vivid life. Then suddenly I saw that a shimmering life-line stretched from Bin's brain to my own, down which rapid electrical pulsations were flowing.

'Yes, that is what I wanted you to notice,' said Raphael immediately. 'Usually wild animals have no reasoning individual minds. But when they are domesticated and cared for by human beings, they adore and admire them and strive to emulate them. The germ of mind is fertilized in them by their human masters. It is actually nurtured and grown in them from the human mind, to which it is attached by a sort of umbilical cord or life-line, as you are now observing.'

'How wonderful!' I exclaimed, 'so that an animal like Bin, or even like an intelligent circus horse, is really growing a mind?'

'Yes, he is becoming an individual and gaining an individual consciousness or soul, instead of or as well as sharing a collective soul with the rest of his kind. Now you can understand what a tremendously important function human beings are meant to have in regard to animals. From humans the animals gain their embryonic minds. That is why so long as men kill each other animals will do the same. For the rays of human mind permeate the thickest jungle just like wireless, and are registered by all living creatures.'

By this time Bin was assailed by a quite human longing for his tea. He came closer to me, stood on his hind legs with his paws on my knees and eagerly and impatiently licked my hand. I gathered him up in my arms and turned to show him to my friend.

But Raphael had gone. He had slipped away in that quick and quiet way of his, almost, I thought, as if he did not want me to observe the manner of his going.

It was some time before we discovered that Fluffy's babies had actually arrived. The little heap of straw which constituted her nest looked quite neglected and she was always rather ostentatiously gazing in another direction. One day, however, I noticed the straw give a succession of little hops. I gently raised a wisp of it, and there beneath was a medley of little soft wriggling bodies. Fluffy sat serenely in the opposite corner, her great eyes entranced, her immaculate white fur standing out around her like a corona. She evidently knew her job no matter how dumb she seemed. But I was quite sure that no magic filament stretched between myself and this half-tame rabbit, who was quite obviously uninterested in acquiring a mind or anything else that humans had. Baby rabbits were the all-in-all of her existence.

Just across the village green lived a man who kept dozens of Angora rabbits. He was a young farmer who was struggling manfully to make a living out of his fertile little farm, in the face of every kind of difficulty, such as shortage or non-existence of labour, misleading or unfulfilled promises by the government, lack of ploughs and other farming necessities.

Harry was usually at his wit's end to know what to do for the best, and he put in a sixteen-hour working day, including weekends. I liked him because he was cheery and helpful and appeared to adore his animals, especially a pair of white goats whose antics he was never tired of watching. One day he invited me to see his hens, of which he seemed proud. I was curious, because I had never seen a hen anywhere on his farm.

He led me to the large dark barn in which I knew the Angoras were housed, and guided me to the far end. As I followed him, I heard the gentle clamour of much clucking. Then suddenly I realized that the whole of the wall at the end of the barn was lined with wire cages, long narrow affairs in which stood scores of hens almost shoulder to shoulder. There was no room for them to turn round. Their food was arranged in a narrow gutter in front of their beaks. Their eggs fell onto the wire netting. They led a completely robot existence – food in at one end, eggs out at the other. They never saw the sun or scratched the earth.

'Its very easy to collect the poultry manure this way,' announced Harry proudly. 'Oi can let you 'ave as much as you loike!'

I felt utterly horrified and disgusted.

'Don't you think it is a bit cruel,' I asked the farmer gently, 'to confine these birds as if they were political prisoners? They have done you no harm!'

'See here, Miss!' replied the young farmer firmly. 'If those hens was unhappy I do suppose Oi wouldn't be getting any eggs. But Oi gets far more eggs than Oi would if those hens were runnin' about the way yours is! An' foine proise eggs they is, too! So they hens *must* be happy and healthy Oi'm thinking!'

I knew that it would take hours of arguing to sow a doubt in the honest farmer's mind. Nevertheless those hens and thousands like them were condemned to a life such as would be considered too severe a punishment for the most dastardly of criminals. I felt I never wanted to eat an egg again, now that I knew what intensive egg production really was.

'Would you loike to see me *bull?*' asked Harry impressively, as if he were about to grant a special favour.

'I didn't know you had a bull – I've never seen it anywhere!' I exclaimed in astonishment.

The young man turned and led the way past the barn to an outhouse just behind, of which I had noticed that the door was always closed. He opened the top half of the door and I looked in. In the darkness of the narrow interior there loomed up the majestic figure of an enormous bull. He moved heavily towards us, snuffling the air, his small bloodshot eyes glaring anxiously at us, his great muscles rippling under the glossy skin. There was a ring through his nose and he was chained to the wall.

'Best bull Oi've had in years, he be!' remarked Harry contentedly.

'Yes, he's grand!' I agreed, 'but its a lovely sunshiny day – when is he going out in the meadow? He can hardly turn round in this dark little place!'

'Lor'! Miss, you could'nt let *him* out into the meadow! He'd be far too much trouble. He fattens up better 'ere, and then he's quite ready every time I want him to serve a cow! That's the only time *he* goes out!'

I felt rather sick. So this magificent animal was condemned to a life of solitary confinement and darkness to suit our convenience! I felt I never wanted to eat beef again and be a party to such cruelty. For a long time now I had been a half-hearted vegetarian, but after this I felt the challenge was too great for my conscience.

'But where are your calves, anyway?' I asked the farmer suddenly. 'I don't think I have ever seen any!'

'Oh, Oi've got some little beauties! You come along here!' And he led the way to some more cowsheds at the rear. I peered into the dimly lit interiors and saw one exquisite little calf after another, standing alone and expectant upon the sparse straw.

'But don't *these* go out into the meadows either? And why aren't they with their mothers?' I asked in bewilderment.

'We foind they fatten up better in 'ere' explained Harry. 'And it wouldn't do at all to leave them out with the mothers – Oi would'nt have enough milk to sell. They calves will fatten up foine in here and Oi'll get quite a good proice for them in a little whoile. Then you'll get your veal, maybe, unless it goes to the army!'

'I see!' I said bitterly. 'It doesn't seem much of a family life, for the bull, or the cow – or the calves! A poor return for all the service they give us!'

Harry gazed at me with a puzzled frown, trying to understand what I meant. And I began to feel foolish, realizing how ignorant a town-bred creature such as myself could be about ordinary country life.

'But what about *me*, Miss?' Harry asked at last. 'Oi've got me woife and three kids. Oi can hardly make do as it is! Oi have to do as all the rest do, or Oi'd be a laughing stock! Oi must be able to get me market proice, mustn't Oi? And besides if we started messing about with oideas like yours – why, we'd never win the war!'

'Yes, you do seem to be caught in a trap!' I agreed heavily, feeling that it was unkind to upset the young man who was really only a cog in the agricultural wheel. 'I think you're doing splendidly, and I'd better have a barrow-full of that nice poultry manure, please.'

12

Former Incarnations

I left Harry with his spirits restored and wandered off to
think about my new discoveries. Evidently I had been
too engrossed in my own gardening, so far, to realize what
was going on around me. I still knew very little about the
activities of farm life. Those beautiful little calves with
their gentle playful ways were considered only as *things*
from which you could get meat and money! The dignity
and power of the bull was in continuous humiliation. The
cow was looked upon merely as a living milk bottle! Was
all this *necessary?* Was there really no other way?

I remembered the words of Raphael, the reference he
had made to Genesis. I turned and hurried back to the
Grange, and went upstairs to my room. From my bookshelves I unearthed my rather neglected Bible and opened
it at the beginning. I soon found on the very first page the
instructions which God gave to Adam: 'Behold I have
given you every herb bearing seed, which is upon the face
of all the earth, and every tree, in which is the fruit of a
tree yielding seed; to you it shall be for meat.' On the
second page I found that the Lord God, after arranging
the ideal life for man and woman whom he had created
in the Garden of Eden, said! 'Of every tree of the
garden thou mayest freely eat,' and gave them, as their
work, the care of the Garden.

However, when Adam and Eve disobeyed the laws of
nature and acted contrary to God's plan, their punishment was made plain on the following page: 'Cursed is

the ground for thy sake; in sorrow shalt thou eat of it all the days of thy life; thorns and thistles shall it bring forth to thee.' Evidently, I thought, it was a punishment to have to eat anything other than tree-food; and thorns and thistles were also evidently an aftergrowth due to Man's disobedience. I continued reading.

'In the sweat of thy face shalt thou eat bread, till thou return unto the ground.' That seemed to prove that eating bread was part of the punishment and even a cause for early death! I read on, engrossed. I raced through thousands or even millions of years of history in a few pages until I came to the new instructions which the Lord God gave to Noah when he came out of the Ark to begin civilization afresh:

'Every moving thing that liveth shall be meat for you; even as the green herb have I given you all things, but *flesh with the life thereof which is the blood thereof shall ye not eat.*' [Author's italics]

'Every moving thing' must therefore refer to plants and trees, not to animals.

'And surely your blood of your lives will I require; at the hand of every beast will I require it, and at the hand of man; at the hand of every man's brother will I require the life of Man,' the admonition continued. I felt that this meant that a man destroys himself psychologically by the act of murder of animal or neighbour – by suppressed guilt, even if outwardly punished by disease of the blood (premature death). Evidently one was to suffer death if one killed animals. It was apparently just as bad as killing one's fellow man!

Did those ancient instructions in the Bible mean anything? Was it because they had not been followed that mankind was in such a mess today? If there was such a lot to know – all those marvellous things which Raphael had shown me for instance – how could people be expected to find out, when they were mostly too hard-worked, under-educated or wrongly educated, so that they did not begin to realize what there was to know. It all seemed unfair when you considered that more than half the people in the world never had a chance to learn anything worthwhile.

'I see you are continuing your studies without me,' came Raphael's voice over my shoulder as he looked down at my Bible. 'That is just what I have been waiting for. Bravo!'

I sprang up and wheeled round eagerly, a score of questions ready on my lips.

'All right! All right!' smiled Raphael intercepting them. 'I know just the point you have reached! Now, you have written quite firmly about reincarnation, haven't you? Do you believe in it?'

'Well – yes!' I replied carefully. 'Of course I must believe in it because it would explain so much. But I have no real proof, only faint memories.'

Raphael sank down into a chair and prepared to explain.

'You have yourself observed with what a tiny fraction of space, of time, and of knowledge the average man is acquainted. He is quite unaware of much that is going on around him. But he used not to be like this! Ancient peoples were mostly very clairvoyant and knowledgeable about the scientific aspects of life such as astrology, biology and spiritual laws. Throughout much of its history most of mankind believed in reincarnation. But during the Dark Age, the last few hundred years, including today, man has been developing his physical creative powers. He has been engaged on the conquest of matter. You see, if he had preserved his spiritual knowledge he would have been much too happy to battle with matter. His individuality, or soul, has developed through a long succession of lives on this Earth during which one lesson after another is being learnt. The destiny of mankind is very glorious. Men are learning to become gods. "All that I do and more, shall ye do after me!" said Christ, if you remember. But the godlike qualities such as patience, integrity, love, industriousness, and mind-power, can only be learned through suffering, privation, and the varied experiences provided by life upon this planet!'

Raphael paused and looked expectantly at his pupil. I was known to have a rather extraordinary and unfeminine way of trying to keep to the point. So I now asked abruptly:

'*Why* should human beings have to learn to become gods?'

My companion sighed patiently. Then he took my hand and led me to the open window. It was a glorious July evening. The moon shone calmly and the deep blue sky was pricked by millions of twinkling stars.

'Look how they twinkle!' said Raphael. 'Do I have to remind you that they are all alive, that they are all the physical bodies of heavenly beings? Those beings are progressing as well as we are. From time to time one of them matriculates, as it were, and has to move on to more advanced work. His place then becomes vacant. It must be filled by a younger deity. From where does he come?'

'Really, Raphael!' I protested, struggling with this new train of thought. 'You surely are not suggesting that we, here on earth, are in training for the future ruling of some star or other?'

'Well, my dear, what *do* you think happens to some of our wonderful geniuses and saints after they finally leave this Earth? Do you think nothing in particular happens to them? Do you believe that all their special talents and qualities are wasted? Do you imagine that the extraordinary care and thought which has been lavished on designing this planet and all thereon has been for no *purpose* at all?'

I felt a pang of despair.

'I've never thought about such things, and I don't know of anyone who has,' I said, almost sullenly.

'You asked for knowledge,' said Raphael sternly. 'I

have given you the merest hint. Is it too much for you?'

'No! No! But its so – stupendous! And seems so far away from our everyday problems. What bearing has it on humanity's immediate difficulties?'

Raphael suddenly broke into a delightful laugh.

'Really, Verity! You are determined to keep me to the point, aren't you! I do congratulate you on your single-mindedness. You will get somewhere at that rate! Well, now, *this* is the point! Obviously, if man is to become a god he has a long journey to go. This journey has been known of throughout history as "the Path". It has very many stages or steps as the human being gradually un-folds his consciousness, develops his character and shifts his interests from materialism to soul-life. He has so much to learn that he has to come back again and again to this Earth. Each time he is reborn he is tuned into a different key, as it were, by the combination of the Cosmic rays then in action, and therefore has a different lesson to learn and a quality to develop. Would you like me to show you your own past lives as an example?'

'Oh Raphael!' I breathed, astounded, 'but how could you possibly do that?'

'There is one stratum of the ether which we call the Reflective or Akashic Ether,' explained my friend, 'it is photographic and records pictures of everything taking place, and all sounds made. This is impossible for us in physical bodies to imagine. But there are some people who can see this ether, so that when they concentrate upon some object they see pictures of events connected with that object. This gift is known as psychometry. There is a part of everyone's personality which is linked with Akashic Records appertaining to himself. I am going to give you a glimpse of yours.'

Here was something entirely unexpected. I braced my-self for the coming adventure, not having the slightest idea what to expect.

Meanwhile Raphael was glancing around the room.

'Ah, this will do nicely!' he exclaimed, approaching the window and placing his hand upon a large round glass bowl of water, standing on a little table in the full rays of the moon. 'We need something like this on which you can concentrate your gaze until you begin to look inwards through your own aura. Come and sit over here, Verity, and look very quietly and steadily into this bowl.'

I seated myself by the bowl and began to gaze into it. The rays of the moon played through it with mysterious effect so that one could begin to imagine all sorts of things. But just at that point the bowl suddenly seemed to fill with smoke, through which moving figures could be seen dimly.

I pressed forwards, probing the swirling smoke with my eyes. Gradually things became clearer. I was gazing at the inside of a cave. In the corner was a heap of bracken and straw upon which a half-naked woman was lying. Her long matted hair was held roughly in place with a twist of leaves. Two naked babies crawled about the ground, which was littered with bones and shells. The stench of the place was terrible. Presently a man came into the cave. He was dragging part of a freshly killed animal. The woman sprang towards it and began to tear it apart with her fingers. The man cuffed her, and settled down to do the job properly with a piece of flint. The woman seized another piece of flint and begged to be allowed to help. The man pushed her away. She sank down upon the ground and began to draw marks and patterns with her piece of flint in the smooth earth. She was doodling! I strained forwards to look at the marks she was making. There was a triangle with another triangle superimposed upon it and a circle within the two. The woman was absorbed. The man finally came over to see what she was doing. He appeared to be furious, jealous! He began to beat her. Then the scene faded and the bowl was full of smoke once more.

I breathed deeply and looked at Raphael.

'Those were just the same as the doodles *I* do when I am – not thinking!' I stammered.

'Yes, that woman was yourself, many thousands of years ago, but even then you had mystic knowledge stored up in your subconscious from the past. Now look again!'

The smoke had cleared away. I saw the inside of a temple. It was obviously Egyptian. A group of young priests were listening to their teacher, an older man. He was explaining to them the meaning of mystic symbols carved upon the walls – two triangles with a circle within them! There was something familiar about the flashing dark eyes of the priest.

'Yes, that was yourself!' came Raphael's voice, 'and that young student with the blue eyes who is learning so eagerly was your husband of the cave!'

The scene changed again. Now there was a feast in progress. A gay group of people were lying about upon low couches. Their manners were far from decorous and their heads were garlanded with flowers. It was a scene of debauchery, and in the leading spirit I once again recognized myself. Several of the other faces seemed very familiar also. Was one of them my sister? One my father?

The scene clouded over again. I had been quivering in disgust, but before I could express my feelings a quite different life was unveiled before me. A mean dark street, down which came the melancholy tinkle of a bell. The bell belonged to a bowed and broken figure horrifying to the eye. He was a leper. He crawled painfully towards a house on the right and waited. The door opened and two people looked out, pityingly, and placed a parcel of food upon the ground. Once again I thought I recognized my father and my sister. And the leper was – myself! He came forward to pick up the parcel and gazed from a distance longingly upon the inmates of the house. He was shut out for ever, he thought.

'In the life before this one,' explained Raphael, 'you had demoralized your family. So you had to learn the results of debauchery: an unclean body and a lonely life! But look!'

A priest approached the leper and gave him a talisman upon which was a symbol: two triangles and a circle! The poor wretch fell upon his knees, memories stirring within him. In an access of repentance he flung himself upon the ground; the priest bent and touched him. A miracle took place. He sprang up, healed!

'He learned his lesson quickly in that life. He will never give way to sensuality again – that is one more step upon the Path,' whispered Raphael as the scene faded and changed.

'He – he – was me!' I stammered, bemused. 'I have often been a man then?'

'Of course! Each developing soul needs the benefit of every available experience. Also, each one has his own group of fellow-souls to which he belongs, and with each of whom he experiences a variety of relationships. He who was your husband in one life, was your priestly acolyte in the next. Your mother may have been your child in a former incarnation. The soul itself is without sex and without age, except in the maturity of experience and of attainment.'

But now there was a scene of much splendour within the glass bowl. A feudal castle, with a duke and his duchess seated in a glittering state room, holding court. I was quick to realise that the duchess was myself. My heart gave a great leap when I looked upon the face of the duke, for he was none other than my fiancé, dead these last six years. There could be no mistake. The same gentle grey eyes and delicate distinguished features! He was looking at his duchess with the devoted expression I remembered so well. Alas, the duchess looked proud and contemptuous. She seemed too sure of him, and had ceased to value his love. Instead, her gaze wandered continuously to one of the courtiers who had a merry laugh and flashing blue eyes, eyes which I had already noticed in some of the other scenes. This eager young man appeared to have made dangerous enemies at court because of his enthusiasm over some progressive and humane improvements in social conditions which were being suggested to the duke. I could observe the friends and favourites of the duke influencing him against these new ideas, and trying to encompass the young man's disgrace. The duchess protected the young man vigorously, even though so doing meant that she should take sides against her husband.

The scene changed rapidly. Tired of the intrigues and shallowness of the court, the duchess had forsaken her husband and escaped with the young courtier. They fled on horseback but they were both killed by the duke's friends who pursued them.

As this scene faded out I turned to Raphael in puzzlement.

'I was in love with both those men, wasn't I? And they were both in love with me? Who, then, was my real husband – my true mate?'

'Could you face the idea that a person's real affinity is a *group* and not an individual, and that he bears various relationships in successive lives to the members of this group, of whom each one only supplies one aspect of his psychic needs? Towards the end of a person's evolution he finds and recognizes all of his own group. He then experiences psychic completeness – full creative expression, and he is never lonely again.'

'I recognized that duke!' I confessed. 'He was my fiancé Raoul in this life. I think Raoul's death was caused by his being so much under the influence of his family. It has taken me years to get over it.'

'He was under the influence of those same people when he was the duke,' replied Raphael. 'But instead of helping him to become stronger, you, as the duchess, despised him! That is why you had to lose him in this life, when you had come to value him!'

'I *see*,' I said. 'There was some justice in it then. But the

young man with the blue eyes? I have not met him anywhere in this life yet.'

'You will,' answered Raphael quietly. 'He has yet to
repay you for your championship of him in those feudal
days. Although you were both killed, you had encouraged
in him a permanent devotion to progress, and human
welfare. That was the beginning of much future work
together.'

'Future?' I echoed wonderingly. 'I have been feeling
as if I had settled down to a lonely end of my life, hidden
away in the heart of the country here!'

'Even if that were so,' retorted Raphael, 'what is one
little life amongst the many that are yet ahead of you?
It is merely a moment in time. You must learn to have a
different attitude towards time, you know. It has taken
you, personally, several million years, remember, to get to
the point when you really want to know why you are here
on Earth at all!'

'Yes, it seems terribly slow progress,' I murmured
regretfully. 'How patient I will have to be!'

'How patient *others* will have to be,' cut in Raphael,
'who are either training you or awaiting your services to
the world.'

'Which others?'

'I am merely referring to the Hierarchy', said my
teacher somewhat acidly. 'Cherubim, Seraphim and all the
Company of Heaven! They cannot get on without you.
If they could you would not be here. Every human being
with the *will* to progress is of great importance to the
Plan. But here we touch upon mysteries too deep for you
to consider as yet. Let us return to our present studies.'

I was about to ask a hasty question, when I suddenly
caught sight of Raphael's face within the glass bowl. Very
astonished, I bent eagerly forward. The scene which was
unveiling before my eyes was a sombre one. It was the
interior of a dark and gloomy prison in which several
groups of people were clustered. With a thrill of horror

I knew a stab of memory. I did not need to be told that I was looking upon a scene in the French Revolution, and that all these people were awaiting the guillotine. The figure of Raphael stood out amongst the rest for he appeared proud and unafraid, although his eyes were flashing with anger and exasperation. A tall young man was pleading earnestly with him. My knowledge of French enabled me to get the gist of what he was saying. 'You *must* be spared!' he was pleading. 'All those people, who are having such wonderful teaching from you, will slip back into the old ways if they lose you. I am of no account, a useless young man! Let me wear your priestly garments and impersonate you at the guillotine – see, I already have a beard! My family's escape is arranged for and you can easily pass for me if you are wearing my coat!'

'It is true,' replied the priestly Raphael gravely, 'that I have *very* important work to do at this time, but this would be a bitter way of achieving it!'

'You know also that I cannot live for long anyway,' the young man continued earnestly, 'because I am tubercular. Instead of the lingering death which faces me, if indeed I escape Mère Guillotine, will you not give me the great privilege of aiding you now, after all you have done for me?'

At this moment there was a disturbance at the door of the prison which opened. The guards began to call out the names of those who were to prepare for their last journey. Raphael the priest, was evidently amongst their number. He straightened himself suddenly and began to take the cloak from his shoulders.

'Very well, my dear friend, I will accept your offer,' he said decisively. 'You know that we will return to Earth again before long, and then I will enjoy repaying you for this service. May le bon Dieu bless you for the aid you are now giving to me and to all those in my care!'

The young man sprang forward eagerly to offer his coat and take the cloak. As he turned his head in my direction

I saw that he bore my own features, at least in all that was visible above his beard!

At this I gave such a violent start that the scene in the bowl was shattered. I turned anxiously to Raphael. He was smiling gravely at me.

'Yes!' he said, 'that young aristocrat was yourself in your last incarnation, and truly you did me a greater service than you knew. That is why I am now at your disposal and am continuing your training from where we left off in those dark days in Paris.'

'Raphael!' I began thoughtfully, 'in that last life I was a man and rather different from what I am now. But you – you do not seem to have changed at all! Only your cloak is missing!'

My companion paused for a long time. Apparently he was considering how much to tell me.

'Perhaps,' he said quietly, 'I really have not changed since then!'

'What do you mean? Surely you are not trying to tell me that you are the same person? That reminds me of what you said about people living for 200 years!'

I broke into an amused laugh, but suddenly checked myself and gazed at Raphael intently. His deep and beautiful eyes responded to mine quite calmly.

'Raphael, I've always realized that you are not an ordinary man! You have shown me so many marvels. You come and go almost magically! Your very presence makes me feel that life is wonderful. Who are you? *What* are are? Are you 200 years old? But you look youngish – and strong! Are you – are you – one of the Hierarchy?'

'And if I told you that I *am* one of the Hierarchy, what would that mean to you? Tell me!'

'Well – I – er – don't really know' I faltered rather helplessly.

'And I don't expect you to know!' exclaimed my friend. 'Your Church doesn't know and hasn't taught you – so how can you know? Nevertheless as the Church upholds the existence of the Hierarchy, it's really up to her to know something about them!'

'I've always understood that the Hierarchy consisted of angels and – saints – and – er – '

'Yes! *I* know! Vague disembodied creatures, beautiful of course, floating about, playing on harps – eh?'

I had to chuckle.

'Well – I – er – '

'All right! If the archbishops haven't got any further than that, we cannot expect much from a mere layman like yourself!' smiled Raphael, 'but oh dear, you *have* a lot to learn. The Hierarchy is the spiritual government of this solar system, and of this planet. They do not float about playing harps. They govern! And very hard work it is too. But their's is not an autocracy. They govern in the *real* way, through *teaching* and cooperation. Their ranks are stepped down from the highest Beings, of whom we cannot even conceive, to the humble saints on Earth who are qualifying sometimes more rapidly than their fellows for promotion upon the Path.'

'Then where do *you* come in, Raphael?' I asked bluntly.

'Oh, how you do keep to the point! But I do not think I can answer you, yet. You must discover much for yourself as you gain more knowledge!'

I continued to regard my teacher with a feeling of doubt, almost of suspicion in my mind.

Raphael was not slow in observing this.

'What is the matter, my friend?' he queried gently. 'Have I done something wrong?'

His compelling eyes forced an answer out of me.

'You say so many startling things that I have no way of verifying – '

'For instance?'

'Well, this question of being able to live for 200 years. Am I really expected to believe that?'

'Listen, Verity! I do not blame you for being ignorant. Practically everyone is! Many generations of wrong living, wrong thinking, wrong feeding, and immoderation in everything to do with the physical senses and the emotions, have so atrophied people's brains and clouded their minds, that only the most rigorous disciplinary measures will repair the damage, and allow them to begin really to think! But actually this question of longevity is no secret. It has been demonstrated by scores of people. I believe in fact that certain books have been compiled containing all the data you might want. Possibly they may be available in the British Museum. Plants, animals and human beings, when given the right conditions, have lived to a very great age. But obviously mankind should be able to beat them all because if he chooses, *he* is the one who has power over his environment and over the other kingdoms in nature.'

I stood up suddenly and walked across to the long cheval mirror in the corner of my room. I surveyed myself earnestly. I had always taken my good looks for granted. We were all a handsome family. We were of that energetic type that continues to look very much less than its age for a long while.

Yet, lately? There had been times when an unexpected feeling of age, of tiredness, or of weakness had suddenly come over me. I had taken but little notice. A few grey hairs! A few wrinkles perhaps? One could have those when one was quite young! But this tired, aching feeling, especially around the heart – this was something new. I had tried to take no notice. But was I, in truth, beginning to grow older?

I faced Raphael.

'I am *already* starting to grow old!' I announced definitely.

'Do you mind?' came one of those trenchant questions of his.

'Well, no, not really,' but that is because I am not sure what there is to live for any more. I have seen two wars this one worse than the first. I lost my fiancé and now my art has been taken from me. I have lived intensely, known heaps of people, and learned *nothing* – until you came! Of course, I have written a book but I recognize that my knowledge was only theoretical. As yet I can hardly realize the implication of all you have shown me. But – but – you have shown me a new world, a much more *real* world! You have given me a reason for wanting to live *long* and learn it all! And now – I suppose it is too late?'

And I turned once more, wistfully, to the mirror.

'Verity!' the voice was gentle but very earnest. 'What would your new reason be for wanting to live long and learn it all?'

I turned swiftly to him, full of enthusiasm.

'Why, to help people everywhere to understand all these things you have taught me!' I replied without hesitation. 'To make them realize about the living planet and all the wrong things they are doing against their own health and progress! To help to open their eyes as you have opened mine!'

'Ah! So you would like to have a new lease of life in order to do that? Well I think I may promise that your desire will be achieved!'

'Raphael!' I breathed in amazement.

'Yes, *but*' – continued my teacher hastily – 'there are certain conditions which must be fulfilled before I can teach you the secrets of a prolonged life. You must prove to me that you are both willing and capable of carrying out your desire to serve humanity through spreading these teachings. And you must also work off some of your own Karma, or destiny, before you will be fit to receive these secrets.'

I was hanging upon his words with rapt attention, trying hard to realize the full purpose of what he was saying.

'I've written about Karma – but what do *you* mean by it?' I broke in.

'Karma is the result of past thought or action. Often it is arranged by the soul in order to develop character.

Suffering, striving, making mistakes – these are the means by which we grow – you know that! I do not have to tell you! In one's relationships with people one has envies, antagonisms, devotions, possessiveness. All these have to be resolved into *love* – impersonal love – before one's mind clears sufficiently to receive not only knowledge but wisdom. You have still many adjustments to make in your life – with people whom you have not even met yet – before I can help you to prolong your life.'

'But – but – ' I stammered, 'that sounds as if it will be a hopelessly long time! I will be *really* old by then!'

'You are already *thousands* of years old!' retorted Raphael. 'Please remember that, and stop thinking in terms of a few years. Now listen! I have come to you seven times at the full moon and I have given you seven Cosmic lessons. I will come to you once or twice more! After that you will have to go on by yourself. You will have to continue to learn by yourself, and you will have to begin to serve your fellow men as you have longed to do. You will also have to work out your destiny with certain people. If you make the grade in all these things – then I can carry your training further on to a very important stage, of which I have given you a hint today.'

I was gazing at my extraordinary friend almost in a daze. He had given me too much to think about.

'Verity,' he said gently, albeit with the well-known twinkle lurking in his eye, 'you asked for it! And now you must manage to cope with it. There is no going back. Knowledge is dangerous, wonderful, and onerous! But I know you are brave and determined. Now, see what you can accomplish before I come again.'

So saying, Raphael placed his hand upon my head for a moment as if in benediction. Then he passed quickly and silently from the room, leaving me to ponder earnestly upon the momentous possibilities he had put before me.

13

The Colonel Digs

Fluffy's little children were the prettiest creatures I had ever seen. Tiny balls of pure white fluff, with ruby-red eyes and absurd tufted ears, they hopped and gambolled all over the hutch in the highest of spirits. There were a round dozen of them, three or four of which paid tribute to their hare father by having shorter fur like Bin.

One August morning, however, I saw to my distress that Fluffy had inadvertently sat upon one of her progeny and squashed him into helplessness. The poor little thing was lying upon its side, its hips flattened, incapable of movement. I gathered it up tenderly in my hand – it must have been the size of a mouse without its fur – and carried it carefully back into the house. It was moving its head feebly, but I did not have much hope of saving its life. I tiptoed into the kitchen, not wishing to disturb Marion's siesta upstairs. I popped the little rabbit into one of the side ovens of the big range, so that it was warm enough whilst I decided what to do next. Then I heard loud thumps from upstairs, like somebody hammering.

'Marion must be awake after all!' I thought. 'It is tea-time – later than I imagined.'

I slipped upstairs in my rubber-soled shoes, making no sound. As I rounded Marion's open door a curious sight met my eyes.

Bin, who usually slept peacefully at the foot of Marion's bed until she awoke at about four o'clock and put the kettle on, had become thirsty and impatient. His mistress was oversleeping and he wanted his tea. Accordingly he had gone to the fireplace, seized one of the fire-irons in his strong little teeth, and dragged it across the floor, thumping it up and down as he went. He managed to make quite a din, pausing every now and then to look across at his tea-maker to see if he had awakened her.

I was speechless with astonishment. I too, peered at Marion in the dim light, and suddenly realized that she was, in fact, awake, lying with sparkling eyes watching Bin's thoughtful performance.

Finally she sat up. 'Bin! Bin! What *are* you doing?' she called. The little hare tossed his ears and did a delighted pirouette. His manoeuvre had succeeded.

'Is that you, darling?' Marion said, suddenly observing me. 'Did you see what Binny did! That's the second time he's done it. I couldn't believe it yesterday, so today I just watched him after he awakened me!'

'Yes, I *saw* him! And people say that animals can't think, Bin was doing quite a bit of calculating! I wish Fluffy was more intelligent though. I'm afraid she's nearly killed one of her babies. I've put it in the oven to keep warm.'

Marion sprang off her bed, her maternal instincts aroused, and hurried downstairs. The sight of the poor little maimed scrap of fur roused her fighting instincts. She held the baby rabbit against the warmth of her heart and crooned over it. It was I who had to make the tea and administer it. I then went back to my gardening, leaving the drama unfolding between a little crushed Angora who wanted to die and a fierce human who was going to save it somehow.

The mother hen was taking up a lot of my time these days. The baby chicks had all turned out to be white Leghorns. Trim, neat, and flawlessly white, the tiny birds were quite a revelation to me. They became so used to me that they were inclined to treat me as a large mother hen. I had taken the habit of sitting on a wooden box amongst them with my sketchbook. They used to perch all over me, tucking their little heads into my overall pockets or under my arm in substitute for their mother's feathers. They would stand upon my shoulder or my knee, and go through a most scrupulous toilet, combing each one of their baby feathers with expert care. They were full of intelligence, playfulness and life. I realized that if I were to make pets of any of them I would arouse a most satisfying response. Probably in one or two of them the germ of mind might flow from my own mind to theirs, and abnormal fowl genius would be the result. Obviously that was what happened in the case of waltzing horses, counting dogs, and performing seals. They each had little embryonic minds sprouting from their masters' controlling intellect. Even now, Marion, back at the Grange, might be implanting a little mind-seed in the baby Angora, and thereby taking on a fresh slavery on her part.

At this thought I hurried back to the house in some concern. But it was too late! Marion had warmed a little milk and found a fountain-pen filler. After half an hour's gentle battle with destiny she had won her victory. The baby rabbit was wriggling weakly at the end of the glass tube, sucking for all he was worth. Marion's face was joyful and absorbed. The slavery had begun. For this performance had to be gone through at very frequent intervals.

Unable to deflect Marion's attention for a single second I departed once more to the garden, for there was much to be done. The rich, warm, droning August days were hastening everything from the growth to the ripening. The tall rows of sweet corn rustled more loudly every time one approached them. For the cobs were becoming hard and the leaves were crispening. As for the plum trees, the laden branches beckoned enticingly. But oh, what a lot of work they claimed. The picking, the selling, the storing, the bottling or the drying! And if you left the fruit until it was nicely ripe, it was a toss-up whether the birds or the wasps or the rodents got it before you did. There had been three beautiful figs hanging high up on the barn wall. The birds devoured one of them, the mice or rats from the barn had the second one, whist the third hung there apparently intact. I climbed a ladder to fetch it down. When I plucked it I discovered a score of wasps gorging themselves inside. In former days I would have dropped it hastily with an imprecation. Now, however, I found that my dislike and fear of wasps had left me. I carried the fig, wasps and all, down the ladder and began very carefully to shake the wasps out of it. Finally, only one obstinate insect remained.

'Come out of it, sweetheart!' I commanded gently. It's my turn now! I want a bite too.'

Finally I coaxed the drunken wasp out with my finger and watched him floundering away, in some puzzlement.

'I called him *"Sweetheart",*' I murmured, 'just the same as I do to Bin – or even to Marion! That's very strange! I used to *loathe* wasps and was glad to kill them! Now I feel quite differently. I cannot forget all the marvellous life and activity existing in even a wasp. I cannot forget that a wasp, part of the planet – is also part of the God-life of the planet. And I don't *care* if the wasp stings me! After all, people who kill and eat animals *should* be stung and eaten by insects – it seems only a fair exchange! Well! How much a little knowledge can change one's attitude.'

I stood, the luscious fig forgotten in my hand, and gazed ahead through the glowing, shimmering garden, across the meadow, away to the woods beyond. But I really saw nothing of it all. I saw instead a vision, a sudden revelation, of what life could be like, if people were to live as the intimate servants of nature instead of only as ignorant exploiters.

Next day the army turned up again. The men had been away on manoeuvres. They swarmed all over the Grange and the grounds, and took up their life once more just where they had left it off. They seemed very glad to be back. One by one they slipped up to Marion's little room to tell her their news. Every time I passed by her door, there seemed to be a different bit of the army inside. Either it was a batman, or a doctor, or a sergeant major, or a bandmaster! Even a general had been known to perch himself on the end of the little divan and enjoy a chat and a smoke, the while his polished boots reflected the anxious scrutinizing whiskers of Bin.

One day at last I found Marion alone, busily rummaging in her chest-of-drawers.

'I must say, Marion, you *have* been holding court!'

She turned a pink face towards me.

'Darling, have you such a thing as a piece of *calico?* Its for Bill – he wants to embroider a traycloth for his best girl!'

Bill was an enormous, thick-necked young Samson, a batman, and the pride of the regimental football team. He was shy and short of speech, a very rough type.

I gazed at Marion with admiration.

'I could go up the village and buy a bit?' I hazarded.

'Oh dear no! That would offend him if he found out! Wait a minute – what's this? If I cut the end off this – it might do!'

'Whatever is Bill going to embroider?' I asked. 'I can't imagine him managing to hold a needle!'

'It's to be the regimental crest! And a very complicated one it is, too. He and his girl are going to get married soon – she looks very sweet from her photograph.'

I went musing down the stairs, passing a most disreputable looking tough, who was evidently another batman trying to slip up quietly to see our popular Marion. I felt a wee bit out of it. So much of my time and strength was taken up with my gardening and I was so absorbed in my secret life with Raphael, not to mention my books, that I seemed rather aloof from the army men. I was too young to treat them maternally as Marion did – and not young enough to want to captivate any of them.

Outside on the lawn I saw the colonel who was in charge of all our district. He was a young-looking colonel with a monocle and a bicycle. He was shy and rather charming and slashed his cycle all over with his cane whilst he spoke, in his access of shyness.

'Oh! I say – ah – er – good afternoon! Er – I hear you asked one of my men if he could do a bit of digging for you?'

'Oh yes, colonel, up in the walled garden I meant! But he hasn't time! I'm sorry if I . . . .'

'The lazy beggar! They're all lazy! But – ah – if you like – I mean – I – er – awfully good exercise, you know! I mean, digging! And a chap gets awfully bored doing a colonel's job you know! Always on his best behaviour, what? Never a chance to get his coat off? I mean, if you think *I'd* be of any use?'

The cane was slashing wildly at the poor cycle.

'Do you mean,' I asked gropingly, 'that *you* would like to dig for me?'

'Most awfully! That is – er . . .'

'But of course, it would be an enormous help – but can you really dig?'

'Try me!' and the colonel, using his cane as an imaginary spade, gave such a fierce dig at the inoffensive grass that his monocle fell out with a shiver.

I bounced into my cousin's room that evening, hot and perky.

'Well, Marion, you may have the whole British army up here, on and off, but I've got the colonel – and working for me, too!'

'Well you *are* a dark horse!' declared Marion when she had heard the whole story. 'So he's going to start digging for you tomorrow! I must certainly go and have a peep.

But now, do watch my little invalid taking his meal.'

Marion lifted the baby rabbit from his wool-lined box, and grasped him firmly round the middle. He was kicking out wildly as he watched her other hand approaching with the fountain-pen filler full of milk. He flung himself upon it and almost swallowed it whole, kicking and sucking in the most frenzied delight. He was growing almost visibly. His sharp little red eyes were like rubies in his fluffy white face. He had begun to follow his big mistress all round the room like a friendly mouse. Bin was quite intrigued too, and sometimes gave the youngster a lick and a polish in passing.

But I shook my head over it all. 'What will Bin do when baby grows up? There'll be a fight. Much better let the little thing go back to his brothers and sisters whilst there is still time,' I begged.

Marion's face fell pathetically. In her heart she also had anticipated this inevitable sequel.

'All that patch there!' I said to the colonel, pointing out a corner of the walled garden which had entirely got the better of me, and looked like a miniature jungle. 'It all wants deep digging!'

'Marvellous!' cried the colonel, his monocle glittering. 'Simply marvellous! What *exercise*! I say, do you mind if I really get down to it – I mean, take off some of these frightful trappings you know?' and he indicated his uniform.

'Take off whatever you want to!' said I promptly as I settled down to weed my onion bed, whilst I watched proceedings out of the corner of my eye.

Off came the colonel's belt and tunic. Soon the apple trees were festooned with his garments, whilst he, stripped to the waist, was wading happily into the thistles and nettles and working havoc amongst them, his hair standing on end and his monocle apparently lost for ever! By the time Marion arrived he was completely unrecognizable.

'I bet he's done better than any of his batmen could!' I declared proudly, showing off a patch of digging that looked like a bomb crater.

'Not got into my stride yet!' threatened the colonel. 'Just wait till tomorrow!'

But the next day, alas, the colonel appeared at the front door immaculate as ever, but with a grave face.

'Shan't have any more time for digging, I'm afraid,' he said. 'We've been ordered to the Front – we shall embark in two or three weeks – exact date's a secret!'

I looked up into his clean-cut, sensitive face. I had been thinking about him quite a lot. He was most attractive.

'I wonder if you'd do something for me, Miss Verity?' he asked suddenly, and slashed fiercely at the doorpost with his cane. 'My Missus – my wife! A bit hard on her when she hears we've embarked you know – I wondered if – I've seen those jolly portrait sketches you do – and er –' (slash!) (slash!) 'my own ugly mug! – the Missus likes it, bless her – Oh, well, never mind . . .'

'Oh, do you mean you want me to do a sketch of you for her?' said I as light dawned. 'Why, of course I will!'

'Oh but its a commission, you know – ah, I mean, only a poor colonel's pay, of course, and a mug like mine, not worth much anyway, what?'

And so it was arranged. I worked every day at the colonel's portrait. My heart was a bit heavy. After the army had gone I would be still more lonely than before.

I pulled myself together angrily. What was all this nonsense when I had been given such marvellous and important work to do by Raphael. Was I indeed unworthy of it? How could I even think of loneliness!

With determination I concentrated my mind upon preparation for his next and last visit. He had told me what he expected of me. I was to begin to find out how to go on by myself – how to win my spurs in the work for humanity which I was determined to do. It would need all my wits and all my courage to make a start. But I was receiving letters almost every day from readers of my first book. I had no excuse. How should I begin?

14

I Begin My Campaign

'You're becoming very fussy about your food dear,' Marion grumbled to me the following evening. 'First you won't eat our nice little loin of pork, and now you don't want chicken! Its weeks since I was able to get a chicken – we are lucky to have any meat at all these days, it seems! And with all the hard work and digging you're doing, I don't think you eat enough. Don't you like my cooking any more?'

'Oh, yes, darling, its better than ever!' I declared hastily, looking longingly at the succulent steaming fowl upon the table. 'Its just that I – oh, well, when you *live* with all these animals, it seems somehow so barbaric to eat them – don't you think so, Marion?'

Marion firmly placed a large portion of chicken upon my plate.

'Now I don't want to hear any more of that nonsense!' she said decisively. 'God gave us the animals to eat, surely? What do you want to live on – carrots? I do hope you are not going to turn into a really cranky spinster – vegetarian and all that sort of thing! That would be the last straw! Here I've spent hours preparing you a really good meal – do I have to eat it all by myself?'

I slowly picked up my knife and fork and began to eat. It was delicious, all of it. Marion chatted cheerfully on, watching me with surreptitious concern. Raphael's words streamed through my mind. The verses in Genesis danced before my eyes. I was bewildered, torn in two directions. I was hungry and yet I was revolted. Whatever should

I do? It was true enough that the few vegetarians I had met seemed to be a bit cranky, weedy and obsessed with their particular cult. I did not want to become like that. But perhaps they would have been like it anyway, or even worse, leading a different sort of life. But what was Marion saying?'

'. . . the postman's wife – so sad, she is going to die of cancer. It will probably be agonizing. Nothing can be done. She hasn't been told, so he has to bear the news all alone. I hardly knew what to say to comfort him. *Such* a nice woman too!' and Marion sighed resignedly.

'People are dying like flies in this lovely district, and no-one has the faintest idea why, or tries to find out!' I cried hotly. 'We certainly don't need the war to polish us off! Haven't there ever been any really healthy people and couldn't their habits have taught us anything?'

'The medical profession are a wonderful body of men,' retorted Marion loyally. 'I don't know what you and I would have done without them. Of course they do all they possibly can! Now let's go upstairs, it is time for Tommy Handley!'

As I washed up the very greasy dishes, I pondered Marion's last words. If what Raphael said was true, the doctors, who ate the same as everyone else, were also half-witted through poisoning, and could not be expected *really* to understand the situation – of course *that* might be the answer!

'I wish I hadn't eaten that darned chicken after all!' I thought. 'I simply *will* not do it again!'

There was a real heat spell towards the middle of August, although the Essex men had been shaking their heads sadly by the end of June and saying that summer was over. They could almost have been right, but for once their pessimism was defeated. The sun shone and shone. I began to find the heat very tiring. My back ached when

I dug and hoed, my hands ached, my feet ached. I seemed in fact, not to be growing those hard muscles I had so hoped to acquire. Sometimes even my heart ached. It might be sensible to take a little more rest occasionally and then I could plan out the work Raphael expected me to do. So I took the habit of knocking off during the heat of the day and lying in the thick shaded grass under the apple trees with my notebook and pencil. I had decided to send out a printed leaflet touching upon some of the things I had learned, and challenging those people who were interested to get into communication with me. I wondered if I could possibly decide what to write. But, no sooner had I started than the words seemed to flow rapidly and forcefully from my pencil. The things that had been churning at the back of my mind for so long seemed to be sorted out, definite and vigorous.

I wrote and wrote, hardly breathing.

Finally I paused and read it over:

A RALLYING CALL TO PIONEERS
AUGUST 1942

'Many believe that the great battle of Armageddon is at present in full swing; that it marks a crucial point in human evolution; and that at its close a new and better civilization will arise, based on quite different standards of living. It certainly does appear that Humanity must either overthrow the present expression of tyranny and build up a social structure wherein such conditions can never again arise – or be submerged in a wave of self-destruction.

'The success of the forces of tyranny has been due, so far, to their one-pointed determination. We have watched the results of a group of men pooling all their mental strength in the pursuit of one objective (world supremacy) their several minds working as *one mind*, whose composite strength hypnotizes the masses. If those who wished for a just and fair world will follow this plain example, pooling their minds and hearts to work as one coherent unit, their consolidated strength would carry all before it.

'We have to realize that the world is like a great living creature, whose limbs are the continents, whose organs are the nations, whose life-cells are human beings – and in which the well-being of any part depends upon the well-being of every fraction. Throughout the ranks of Humanity outrage is being done to this irrevocable law of unity. This is because so far the great world-body possesses nothing which corresponds to a *mind*, or nucleus of self-consciousness, of sufficient proportions to guide and organize its life as a whole. The human family is one body, whose primary need is for an adequate headpiece.'

I paused in great astonishment.
'Why, but it's *good*,' I whispered to myself, 'I'm sure it's good.'
I continued reading.

'This headpiece should constitute a sort of world government or Council, formed of pioneer experts in every branch of living. In order to begin developing this ideal it is necessary to link together all those of like mind who would be ready to work for it. We want to form a fellowship of pioneers, make them and their ideas known to each other, in the knowledge that Unity is Strength, and that together we may accomplish much that alone we could never do. I therefore appeal to all those who will join hands in this plan, to communicate with me immediately.'

'Of course I must sign it,' I thought. 'And add my address; and then have it printed; and then decide who to send it to. I do wonder if I will get a single answer?'
I was by now feeling exhilarated and excited and anxious to see my leaflet printed. I rushed out of the walled garden and across the orchard and down the drive just as I was, never pausing for breath until I reached the little stationer's shop which undertook printing orders. I had a long session with Mr Pikes, who finally agreed to make a smart little orange two-page leaflet of it, for the modest price of £2.

I retraced my steps slowly. I had taken the plunge. It seemed audacious on my part – perhaps I would be laughed at. But I had to do something very definite as a start. A wonderful picture of the possibilities inherent in all that Raphael had shown me was forming in my mind. My enthusiasm was growing by leaps and bounds. There *must* be others who would join with me. The question was, *how* could I find them?

'Verity, its Tuesday today, you must go to the butcher's for me! Try and do the best you can. Perhaps there may be a little bit of liver today, or you might coax a couple of kidneys out of him! Or even a little sheep's heart!'

Marion's eyes were shining with that keen interest which made her such a good companion in all domestic details. Alas, somehow I could not get up the same enthusiasm. Perhaps I was no homemaker by nature. Perhaps it was the prospect of the butcher's shop which inhibited my interest.

As I trudged up the village street and joined the queue outside the shop I tried not to think of what I was going to do. But it was no use. Raphael seemed to have opened my mind to many things which I had always accepted in the partly-conscious way of habit. Today I knew vividly that I was going to buy pieces of the corpse of a charming animal who had as much right to enjoy life as I had. As the queue moved forward into the shop, I was suddenly confronted with a large new calf's head displayed with pride upon the counter. I looked at it quietly, at its pale smooth cheeks and serenely closed eyes. Suddenly I felt that I couldn't believe it, that it was a nightmare that I and a string of kind-hearted villagers were standing gossiping at the counter whilst the butcher hacked and chopped in front of them.

'Mummy, what is dat?' asked a tiny child, pointing to the calf's head.

'Why, duckie that's a calf's head!' was the reply.

'But Mummy, why hasn't it got any fur?'

'Well, because – because it hasn't! Now don't ask no more silly questions or I shan't buy you your sausage!'

The little child continued to stare wistfully and wonderingly at the calf's head. I escaped as soon as I was served and hurried homewards. But as usual I slowed down when I was passing the meadow where the doctor's Jersey cows were grazing. One of them was standing watching me, her exquisite shape etched sharply against the pale grass. I slipped through the gate. I left my basket on the ground and walked across to the cow, who gave me an interested welcome suggesting that she might like to have her ears scratched. I at once complied, stroking and pulling at the warm soft ears which felt rather like Bin's. The cow snuffled softly and her breath smelt delicious. Her large gentle eyes looked patiently and pleadingly at me from under long fringed lashes. What did she want, was it her calf in the butcher's shop, perhaps?

Chew! Chew! Chew! Quite contentedly. I pressed closer. An intense love for this animal, for all animals, welled up in my heart almost choking me.

'You wonderful creature, I *adore* you, do you hear?' I whispered passionately into the drooping ear. 'You seem to me to be full of heaven, full of – God! Fancy anyone killing, *eating* beings like you! Fancy taking any liberties with you at all! It's a damned impertinence – and I've done it myself!'

'Chew! Chew! Chew!' replied the cow enigmatically.

'Listen,' I continued urgently, 'listen to me! I *promise* that I'll try to make people understand what we are all doing! I *promise* you that I will never take liberties with you or any other animal again! I'll learn to do without exploiting you, somehow! I will spend the rest of my life trying to help people to understand!'

There was the sound of a car along the village road.

I realized that I could not stand indefinitely conversing with a cow – even a Jersey cow!

I seized my basket of hearts and kidneys, with a guilty backward glance at the cow and sped away home.

15

A Glimpse at the Hierarchy

'Marion, darling, come up the garden with me and look at the moon. It's a perfectly glorious night!' I begged as I stood at my cousin's window.

'I'll come with you tomorrow, Verity, I promise! But just now there's a radio play – by Somerset Maugham I think. And Churchill is going to speak to us at nine o'clock – you really ought to be here for that!'

'All right, I will stay until nine o'clock, but then I am going up to the walled garden to see what it is like by moonlight.'

So finally I escaped into the garden with the sombre and urgent words of Churchill ringing in my ears. Blood and sweat and tears were going to win the war – if we *did* win! If not the consequences would be too horrible to contemplate.

'I ought to be feeling roused up to a pitch of frenzied and fanatical endeavour to help to win this war,' I thought, as I opened the gate of the orchard and fastened it carefully behind me. 'But I'm *not*! Is there something wrong with me I wonder? Am I unpatriotic? Somehow I keep feeling that this war is only an *acceleration* of things that go on all the time anyway. People are being killed in their thousands in times of so-called peace, by epidemics, famines, road traffic, and all sorts of accidents belonging to our "modern age". In fact far more have been killed on the roads than in wars. And apart from actual killing, millions are continually being maimed by ill-health, poverty, and many actively poisonous occupations. We all get excited about war because the politicians want us to, but we do not get excited about similar outrages which are done habitually in peacetime because that would not suit the politicians and financiers at all! Oh, I wonder what is the answer to it all?'

The moon was shining calmly and brilliantly down upon the hushed garden. Instinctively I quietened my footsteps as I walked. The mysterious lunar rays imparted a weird cold brilliance to the scene, which made everything seem unreal. Yet there was hidden life on all sides. A cricket was chirping busily in the long grass, an owl was uttering his melancholy hoot overhead, whilst in the distance the bullfrogs were hissing their strange chorus.

The walled garden looked more like fairyland than ever. The pergolas were heavily laden with hanging clusters of pink roses which almost swept the path. The dark old apple trees in the background framed them beautifully, their black shadows flung across the pallid pathways in sinister intensity. The moonlight picked out all the pale swelling Bramley apples until they looked like little moons themselves. Everything was motionless, upright, expectant and entranced. I paused, intoxicated with the beauty and the mystery. Then I crept silently to the old seat beneath the pergola and settled myself down happily to enjoy the poetry of it all.

Why did one love the moon so much? What was it about that cold frozen orb that made the blood flow faster, the sap rise, the tides swing back and forth? There *was* something very special about the moon. What was it? Why, for instance, did Raphael always come at the full moon?

'I want to ask him that now,' I thought suddenly. 'Oh, Raphael, where are you?'

'Here!' came the cheerful reply, as a tall figure detached itself from the black shadows ahead. 'I have been waiting for you to call me.'

'Oh, I *am* glad to see you – but tell me how you get in?

I always keep the garden door locked because of the army.'

Raphael seated himself on the bench beside me. It creaked under his weight. He was real enough – and yet . . .

'Now let me see, where were we?' he asked ignoring my question entirely. 'How much have I been able to teach you so far of that which you wish to know?'

'Oh what a question!' I, his student, was somewhat staggered. 'Shall I ever be able to answer it? Ah, I can see from your face that I *must!* Well of course, you have shown me masses of wonderful things, but I think the most important knowledge I have gained is the realization of the position that humanity is meant to hold in regard to the planets and to the plants and animals; and that if we live properly we would be healthy, and understand how to organize living conditions in the ideal way – but, Raphael! Supposing a great many people *were* to try to live correctly, they would soon be up against all the vested interests in the world! All the people who make their money through wars, or adulterated food, or meat, or alcohol, or tobacco, or betting, or on the Stock Exchange – no-one could ever prevail against all those powerful interests! Not to mention continual rivalries between nations! How could it ever be possible to get the world as a whole to live the right way!'

'My dear Verity,' answered Raphael with a happy twinkle in his eye. 'Why ask *me*, when you have yourself supplied the answer in that very excellent leaflet you mapped out? Let's have a look at the copy.'

Dumbfounded, I hastily fetched the copy from my cabin, amazed as always at my friend's uncanny knowledge.

'But – but – how do you know what I've written?' I stammered, as I spread the copy out on my knee.

My companion produced a businesslike torch from his pocket and at once pointed with his beautiful slender hand to the sentence in question, and I read it out:

'The human family is one body whose prime need is for an adequate headpiece. This headpiece should constitute a sort of world government or Council, formed of pioneer experts in every branch of living!'

'A world government!' I repeated. 'Yes, I know I wrote it, but surely it is what you call a "pipe dream" – it couldn't ever really happen?'

'When you wrote it you were convinced that it *is* the only solution, weren't you?'

'Oh yes, I am still sure it is the only answer – but will it ever come?'

'When enough people are sure, and use their influence, then it *will* come,' replied Raphael quite simply.

'How do you *know?*' I demanded urgently.

'I know because it is part of the Plan.'

Once more I thrilled to that word.

'You mean the Plan of Evolution – the Hierarchy's Plan? But how – how did I guess it?'

'Come with me and I will show you!'·

I rose without hesitation to follow my teacher, moving so naturally that it was some seconds before I realized that I had left my physical body seated upon the bench.

Suddenly Raphael paused and looked back.

'It is going to be cold for your body on the bench in the night air. Go back and instruct your elementals to keep it thoroughly warm until your return.'

I hesitated, swaying doubtfully.

'But – I – er –I?'

'Go on! Hurry!' came the stern command.

Nervously, I went back to my body and looked into its luminous teeming depths.

'Will you keep me warm please, until I come back!' I muttered, feeling rather a fool.

A quivering ripple of life seemed to answer me and gave me a sudden feeling of authority. I hurried back to Raphael, who was standing chuckling at me.

'It takes a bit of getting used to, doesn't it?' he said. 'But people could do a great deal with their bodies if they would only take the matter seriously. Now tonight we are going to have a very strange experience, so you must pay great attention. We are going to share in the dream of another person. Follow me!'

We moved very swiftly so that I had no time to observe our direction. Presently we entered a house and were soon standing in a large sleeping apartment. Upon the bed a fine-looking middle-aged man was lying with clasped hands and closed eyes. Suddenly there was a quivering movement and the man had stepped out of his body just as I could do. He was standing regarding us.

'May we come with you?' Raphael asked him. He nodded his head. Together we all three floated from the room, rising up through clouds of astral substance which moved like mist or fog around us. I was astonished to see many other people journeying in the same way in their astral bodies, their shining life-lines stretching down behind them. Some of them were having vivid experiences. The fog seemed to form itself into the semblance of places, according to the thoughts projected upon it. These activities were easily recognizable to me as dreams.

'Why didn't I see all this when I journeyed before?' I whispered, tugging Raphael's arm.

'Because we were concentrating upon other things and your eyes were otherwise focused.'

We had now passed into a great hall where many of the dreamers were already assembled. They were all earnestly occupied, studying from volumes which they took down from the many bookshelves, or being instructed by companions who accompanied them.

Suddenly I caught sight of cousin Marion amongst the crowd. She was studying from a very large volume and there was someone leaning over and helping her. Her aura was bright with interest.

'Who is helping Marion?' I whispered to Raphael.

'A beloved sister of hers who died many years ago,' was the reply, 'but come! We have to follow our friend.'

Although bewildered by the thrilling interest of the scene through which we were passing, I forced myself to concentrate upon following my two companions. The middle-aged man passed rapidly through the hall and into a private ante-chamber where a great crystal globe was placed beneath a pearly ray of light. He seated himself by the globe and bent his gaze upon it.

'He chooses to learn in the visual way,' whispered Raphael. 'He will allow us to share his vision because he is a friend of mine.'

So saying he drew me softly towards the crystal globe and we all three gazed into it. The familiar astral smoke was already curling within the globe when there came a slight interruption. I raised my head and saw that a young man had just come into the ante-chamber and, slipping quickly into place beside Raphael, composed himself to study developments. Not a word was spoken, nor had I a chance to see his face. So I also bowed my head once more over the luminous globe which was now alight with life in its shifting depths. It seemed as if we were gazing into a large and lofty theatre with a domed roof. A number of people were very intent upon the work they were doing, which looked most complicated.

A large model of the earth was revolving slowly upon a pedestal in their midst, and it was with this that they were absorbed. Some of them had maps and charts swung upon easels which they could wheel from place to place to compare notes. The dome of the theatre was slung with models of planets and constellations. From these bodies beams or rays of coloured lights could be projected upon the model of the Earth by the pressing of switches. Along the far wall a row of great charts was suspended, from which several of the people were taking notes. The whole scene was bathed in luminous quivering light and even the people themselves seemed almost luminous. They gave an impression of both forcefulness and ethereality which I had never experienced before.

Raphael was whispering quietly in my ear.

'Those great charts are indications of the Plan! They contain outlines of future world government and many other wonderful developments which you must not know of just yet. The people you see here are highly privileged. They are amongst the wise ones of the Earth. Some of them are still "alive" as you call it, and visit here in their sleep. Some of them are no longer mortal but help humanity from non-physical spheres. At present you see them studying astrology. They are trying to ascertain conditions affecting different parts of the world and different individuals this month, with a view to disseminating ideas and ideals leading towards the Plan. They get these ideas across by means of dreams, telepathy, books, so-called "inspiration" and so on.'

'And who,' I asked, 'drew those charts of the Plan in the first place?'

'The great ones who have humanity in their care – known as the Masters of the Wisdom – those who have achieved on the Path of which I spoke to you, and who have acquired comparative perfection after many incarnations. Some of their former lives would be familiar to you – such names as Leonardo Da Vinci, Swedenborg, Pythagoras – might be continuing their teaching with many fine souls who work perhaps in obscurity on Earth, and who faithfully perform unpleasant and thankless tasks for the good of human evolution.'

'I can see someone who looks astonishingly like Hitler over there – talking earnestly to someone like Roosevelt. Surely – '

'There are things of which you may not know just yet,' interrupted Raphael passing his hand quickly across my eyes, 'and our studies are over for tonight. Look, our companions are ready to leave.'

I pulled myself together, as the wonderful scene began

to be obscured from my view. Once more I remembered that I had been looking into a great crystal globe. I raised my head and suddenly met the eyes of the young man who had joined our studies. They were of a brilliant dark blue and flashed with a kind of recognition as they met mine. I turned anxiously to Raphael.

'That young man!' I whispered. 'May I speak to him? I seem to remember him – '

'You two often go to the same places to study in your dreams. One day you will meet in the flesh. Let us hope you will be wise on that day!'

As these rather solemn words were spoken I looked round to see that the young man was moving away engrossed in earnest conversation with our middle-aged companion.

'We will leave them now. My friend does not expect any thanks for his courtesy in sharing his vision with us. It is thus that the more advanced ones help those who have not yet mastered the science of meditation.'

As I puzzled over these words we left the ante-room and passed swiftly through many teeming scenes of activity which I once again recognized as the dreams of others.

'Are they *real*, all those scenes we are passing through?' I enquired anxiously.

'In a sense, yes! The mind is a modelling instrument which manipulates this primal astral stuff in the way you would make a plasticine model – only instantaneously, as if with electrical magnetism. It is difficult to explain when you are only used to the physical, solid world. But now wait! Here is some unused astral vapour. *You* shall make something yourself! Do a model of Bin, for instance! Go on! Think of him very hard!'

It was not difficult to picture my beloved little friend. I imagined him steadily, the astral vapour swirling around.

Suddenly I saw the form of the little hare appearing in

its midst. Amazed, I continued nevertheless to concentrate hard. Soon the little body had a quite solid appearance. Even the whiskers were there. Suddenly it *moved!* It gave a joyful little pirouette in the air!

I cried out in a kind of fright – and the little animal promptly vanished.

'What a pity!' remarked Raphael. 'You were doing quite well. You are going to be good at meditation.'

I was feeling very strung up.

'But – why did it *move?*' I had a quaver in my voice.

'As soon as you create any form it becomes imbued with life, usually by an elemental, as I already told you. In this case the form was built by your focusing on Bin's vibrations, so *he* was drawn resonantly, to take possession of it – and thought he was dreaming of you! Ah yes, Verity, there are so many things to be discovered once you break out of your prison of flesh. Without a guide you might think you were going mad – and so would other people!'

'Thank heaven I have you!'

'You will have to do without me very soon. After the next full moon I may have to go away – I have work to do in another country. But you can learn to reach me through the method I have just shown you. Picture me with all the concentration of which you are capable, and you will build a thought-form of me in astral stuff. If you are successful I will be able to use it – almost like a telephone – and answer your questions!'

'I am going to miss you terribly when you go away,' I sighed, 'I think you mean more to me than any friend I have ever had – how long will you be away?'

'Remember what I have taught you about time, my dear,' said Raphael gently. 'I have been your teacher during several of your past lives. I will be your teacher in future lives. It is a bond that will never be broken and it will for ever grow more interesting.'

I clasped his hand between my own. Tears were in my eyes.

'Oh I am so glad – so very glad!' I murmured, 'and I will never forget!'

'Oh yes you will!' responded my friend promptly and surprisingly. 'There will be times when you will forget me altogether, and everything I have taught you! And I will be obliged to leave you to it! You have to learn – everyone has to learn – to be self-reliant in your knowledge and in your work of service. You have to learn to stick to your goal in spite of *everything*!'

'Everything?' I echoed in some dismay. 'Will I encounter a lot of difficulties and troubles?'

'You will,' was the decided answer, 'but remember always that I believe in you and count on you to win through. There are wonderful things ahead if you do!'

I suddenly realized that we were seated upon the garden bench once more, with the moon shining down steadily and calmly upon us.

'Oh I wanted to ask you about the moon,' I begged him. 'Why do you always come when she is full?'

Raphael paused in his careful way before answering, as if he valued the responsibility of teaching me.

'There are many reasons,' he said at last. 'For one thing, when the moon is full she reflects from her whole surface, many marvellous rays impinging upon her from certain other planets. These, striking the Earth at certain angles, produce a condition in the ethers which thins the veil between the material world and the inner worlds. At such times one becomes inspired, mad, or emotional, according to one's make-up. Those who wish to learn wisdom from their own souls or the "higher mind" make use of the full-moon period. They learn to quieten the whole personality, so that they can become aware of the subtler side of life. That, as you know, is called *"meditation"*, and I ask you to practise it steadily from now on, until you learn thus to obtain your own answers to any of your questions! And on the way to that stage, you will also make it possible for *me* to send you messages and ideas.'

'Oh Raphael, so you really think I will be able to?'

'Yes, certainly! Nothing is impossible if you want it sufficiently. "Where your heart is there will your treasure be also", as the wise Master Christ said.'

My friend turned towards me and placed his hand for a moment upon my head as if in blessing.

'Go back home now, Verity, and leave me here,' he said. 'Our study is over for tonight. Carry on with the work you have set yourself until we meet again.'

I rose from the bench, grateful and somewhat overcome by all that I was receiving. Obediently I made my way through the entranced moonlit garden. At the gate I paused, and looked back.

The moon's rays were playing over the silent seated figure of my friend. Skimming down these rays there appeared to be little luminous figures who tossed and danced around the bench. They were coloured like moonbeams and glittered like dewdrops. I suddenly remembered the fairies I had seen in my former experience with Raphael. I started with excitement, but alas, my brusque movement seemed to break the spell. For the little figures vanished, so swiftly that I wondered if I had imagined them.

'Or did I see them with my astral sight?' I asked myself as I continued reluctantly on my journey towards the Grange and away from Raphael. 'I certainly must try and be steady in my practice of meditation. I have neglected it terribly since coming here. I will begin more seriously tomorrow!'

16

Gathering in the Harvest

The colonel's portrait was finished. The colonel, his batman, Marion and I, walked round and round the easel,
cocking our heads this way and that in the throes of final
criticism.

'It's the regular spit of 'im' announced the batman.

'I really do think you've caught his expression, my
darling!' Marion said proudly.

'Well – I mean to say – I think you flatter the old bean
– what? The Missus will fall in love with me all over
again – I say! – what?' cried the colonel, slashing wildly
at the furniture with his long-suffering cane and almost
knocking the easel over.

I cocked my own head and squinted through narrowed
eyes.

'I think I may want to do a little more to the mouth!'

'Well you'll have to look slippy,' said the colonel, his
expression clouding over, 'here today and gone tomorrow,
you know!'

'What? You don't mean to say . . . ?' cried Marion,
scrutinizing him sharply.

'State secret of course! Absolutely dead secret! We have
received our marching orders, but I mustn't divulge the
hour, though.'

The sunshine seemed to pale just then, to Marion and
me. All our soldier friends were going to leave us, like
'ships that pass in the night'. It happened at regular
intervals, but this time it was going to be hard. The war
was at its fiercest, casualties were very high, and 'going

out East' offered many hardships other than the fighting. A cloud settled over the Grange, and under this oppressive melancholy cloud the place seemed like an ant-heap. Heavy boots clattered everywhere. Bundles, packages, guns, were stacked and re-stacked. A continual pilgrimage was going up and down the stairs to Marion's room. Lunch was a sketchy affair. Both of us were distrait. She spent a good deal of time burrowing into her cupboards and drawers, seeking out little things to give to the men, or for them to send to their best girls. I put the last ounce of care and love into my portrait. I felt choked. All these men, so busy and cheerful, were going off to face dirt, pain, sickness and horrors indescribable; all of which they in turn were expected to inflict upon their fellow men – and even, by the bombers, upon helpless mothers and children. And all this because governments could not figure out any better way!

Marion put her head round the door, finger on lips. She was very pale.

'Hush!' she said, 'I found out! They are going tonight at midnight – but the village mustn't know!'

Her eyes were wet and tragic. I regarded her dumbly. There seemed to be nothing to say.

At twelve o'clock that night we two women wrapped ourselves up and slipped out of the house in the wake of the departing men. We went as far as the gate of the drive, and from there we watched them form into marching order in the road outside. All the village slept. There was a misty moon. The scene was vague and mysterious. The men stood silently whilst their young padre gave them a simple address and offered up a short prayer. The young doctor passed down the ranks giving instructions. There was a whispered command. Silently the long line of men melted away into the night, their feet muted in secret departure.

I heard Marion sigh tremulously. I found myself shivering with nervousness.

'Come, darling!' she said suddenly, pulling herself together, 'I think we should go back now and have a *nice* cup of tea!'

'It's three days since Mr Higgs was here,' said Marion next morning. 'He must be ill! You'd better stop at his cottage today and find out. Harry came round just now and offered us 17s. 6d. a bushel for our pears, so they must be picked soon. It's worrying about Mr Higgs. Oh, and will you be sure to get scrag-end of neck-of-mutton for our ration. I want to make a nice Irish Stew – now, you needn't look like that, Verity, *I'll* eat it even if you don't – or I will give some to old Mrs Dobson!'

'Yes, yes, *do* Marion!' said I, rather miserably. 'But I will eat everything except the meat, anyway.'

It turned out that poor old Mr Higgs was down with very bad rheumatism. The doctor said it was through over-work and that he must rest for some weeks. He could only come to us for a half-day's gardening a week, being the last gardener left in the village, anyway!

'Then of course I must pick the pears – but I haven't been feeling too well myself, lately,' I ruminated on the way home. I was interrupted by an excited cry. I looked up to see a curious apparition coming towards me – a young woman mounted perilously upon a bicycle, with an enormous bag swinging from either handlebar, a great bundle on the carrier at the back and another one on the front. Grass and leaves were bursting out of these bags and trailing wisps along the road. It was Thorny. She had been hunting for food along the roadside for her Angora rabbits. She dismounted dangerously but happily.

'I don't like to see you courting disaster!' I reproved. 'You'll have a dreadful accident one of these days, Thorny. You'd much better collect stuff for your rabbits from our garden – there's loads of it!'

The result was that when Thorny arrived to pick weeds she discovered me battling with the garden all by myself and promptly insisted on helping me.

'If our pioneer authoress breaks her back right at the beginning of the story,' she argued, 'well, there just won't be any world government! You must let me help you pick the pears!'

'It isn't only the pears!' I confessed. 'Bin has had about twenty-four children by now. The baby chicks are growing enormously and there are about thirty all-told. They all need a lot of food and exercise and what-not! And as for the garden – why the plum-picking alone would keep a regiment busy, I should think; and then there's all the other fruit coming along, not to mention the vegetables. I just don't know what to do. I love it all, I simply love the work! But there's enough for six people to do here, and everyone in the village is overworked already.'

The next day a young man called to see me.

'Good morning, Miss,' he said briskly. 'I am a worker at the wood factory down the road. Miss Thorn gave me one of your leaflets and mentioned that you needed help in the garden. I don't want any pay, but I thought I would like to give you a hand and hear some more about your ideas – they interest me! But I must tell you first of all that I'm an atheist!' he continued somewhat proudly. 'I don't hold with religion or any stuff like that!'

I looked at him thoughtfully.

'You're an atheist, yet you are interested in humanity's problems, and you are ready to be helpful,' I said. 'That's good enough for me!'

The young man whose name was Pollitt, proved to be a great help to me. All he asked was that he might work close beside me and pepper me with questions. On my part, I questioned him too. It appeared that he had been able to acquire his atheistic ideas from the county council school, in which according to him, no religious instruction was given and most of the teachers had no personal faith either. The basic principle inculcated seemed to be: 'I'm as good as you and without making any effort either!'

I thought it sounded unbelievable, but that it certainly could explain the very uncouth manners which I came across so often in unexpected places.

I spoke about it to Hilda Thorn, and that young woman at once became voluble.

'I went to take some angora wool to Mrs Dickinson yesterday,' she declared. 'She was very unhappy because her pretty new housemaid has left her – such a nice girl too! But it appears that when the girl went over to Letham to the local dance-hall, the men would not dance with her because she is in domestic service! They think she would be a cut beneath them, although most of them are local factory hands. They will only dance with the shop girls, so Betty has gone to get a job in London, where the snob attitudes are apparently different!'

'How amazing!' I gasped. 'One would think a man would *prefer* a girl who is having domestic training, and who would therefore make a much better wife and mother than a shop girl would. I don't understand it!'

'Its all a kind of snobbery, Miss Verity! Working people can be every bit as snobbish as anyone else.'

We were both leaning over the stable door watching the Angora family, as we talked. The young ones were getting quite big now, and were like snow-white balls of thistledown. They bounced and hopped and scattered about most playfully. Their mother looked like a big white cloud as she sat bunched in her corner watching them.

'Fluffy is really ready for clipping now! I ought to take her fur if you will allow me! I have an order to make a baby's bonnet and cape, and it would just do nicely!' said Thorny eagerly.

My permission granted, she soon possessed herself of the outraged and struggling Fluffy. Whipping out a pair of scissors, she began to pull the fur away with an expert touch.

'She doesn't really mind,' she explained to reassure me. 'I did it just before I brought her here. She will feel much cooler afterwards. Of course I don't take all the fur off, I only thin it, as the hairdresser would say! When I pay you, Fluffy will have earned her keep for six months!'

'Well I'm sure I could never learn to do that,' I said positively. 'When the babies are big enough you had better buy them from us altogether. I must reduce the work here somehow. I can no longer manage it at all.'

'I can buy the bunnies from you whenever you want, and I could also buy your young chickens before winter comes,' cried Thorny eagerly. 'Then you would only have the gardening to do, which is more than enough!'

I turned and looked at her quietly.

'Thorny, do you really want any chickens? I believe you would say "Yes" just to convenience me. I believe you spend your whole life helping other people. I believe you really do far more good than I do, for all my great ideas!'

Thorny blushed vividly and shook her head.

'What rubbish' she expostulated, 'you mustn't think like that! I only help people a bit to bear the troubles they've got! But *you* are going to try to help them to avoid the troubles altogether!'

August was over. The rich September days ripened and mellowed. The sunsets became glorious. Everything seemed to be overflowing with repletion, and fruition, and satisfaction. Every note of the little birds expressed contentment, and the bees sounded half asleep. It seemed that I alone had no respite. I was trying to dig up the potatoes. I drove my old friend, the fork, into the soft crumbly earth as hard as I could, hoping to bring the complete harvest of each plant to the surface in one move. I gazed at the firm white tubers with pride. There was good solid food for the whole winter, easy to keep, simple to cook! Oh blessed potato, what could life have been like without you?

My back ached, so did my wrists, and my foot from driving in the fork. I certainly could never dig all the potatoes up. I would have to turn for help to Mr Pollitt. And there were the beets to be dug up and stored, and the celery to be earthed up, and scores of apple trees and plum trees just loaded down with fruit. I sank down upon the soft earth almost in despair. It was all so delightful and satisfying, but I could not manage it. Every day I felt more tired. Every day the weeds were taller and more menacing. Every day the work accumulated.

I began to be afraid. What would happen to the garden if my strength finally failed? Would all my work of the last few years be wasted? It took years to make a garden, but only months for it to go to ruin. And it was all doing so well.

I carefully selected a fine white cauliflower and dug up a bunch of tender carrots to take back to the house for lunch. As I entered the kitchen and placed them upon the table I heard Marion at the outer door having a cheery chat with one of the villagers. When Marion finally came in, I was horrified to see her bearing in triumph a monstrous white cauliflower.

'Where's that come from?' I asked blankly.

'From the market-gardener chap, James Pudney. Isn't it a beauty?'

'Darling, that's the third time recently that I've seen you buying stuff from him! You know we have to economize as much as possible, and that I am breaking my back to produce all we need in the garden. What's the sense of buying from James?'

'Ah, well, you see, I want to get on the right side of James! He can let me have a sack of logs from time to time (I mean, outside of our ration). Think what a help that will be!'

I said no more but I felt rather hopeless. It was extre-

mely difficult to sell any of the produce from our garden.
Most people seemed to prefer to live on meat and tinned
food. None of the villagers would eat salad or spinach or
sprouts. It was impossible even to *give* many varieties of
our produce away. In fact is was extraordinary how few
vegetables most country people seemed to eat.

Marion caught sight of my pained face.

'Now then, you're not going to be sulky, *surely*, because
I buy a few vegetables from poor James? You'll be the
first one to enjoy a good log fire when the cold weather
comes. Really, one can't do anything right these days, it
seems. You'll be telling me next that you don't want saus-
ages for supper?'

'Of course I don't! I've told you six times, darling, that
I don't want to eat any more pork ever again!'

'They only contain a very tiny bit of pork – they are
mostly bread, as everyone knows! You complain about
your backache and you won't eat sensible food. You'll
lose your health at this rate! I'm doing my best for you,
and you only make things difficult!'

Marion sounded on the verge of tears, and I felt very
much like weeping myself. It was all rather difficult. Perhaps I would be wiser to postpone my vegetarian ambition
until the war was over, and no-one was so dependant
upon my company.

'All right, darling,' I capitulated, giving Marion a hug.
'I'll have just one small sausage.'

'Of course you will. I never heard such nonsense!' she
said, brightening up immediately. 'I'll do some nice fried
onions with it.'

17

Raphael's Vision

The beautiful September moon grew larger every night, swelling and shaping like the big yellow egg–plums on the garden wall. I watched this gradual waxing with a feeling of mingled longing and dread. Soon Raphael would come again. But he would come to give me his last lesson. How could I go on afterwards without him? To me, now, he represented the realities of life, whereas my ordinary daily living was meaningless by comparison, meaningless and even unreal. My former way of life had, in fact, often seemed unreal to me in the past: to make money painting portraits: yes, but why? In order to keep myself, to preserve my existence: yes, but what *for?* It was a question I had never dared to ask myself. No-one else seemed to be asking it. They all went on with the daily round and if there would suddenly be time to think, they quickly coped with that uncomfortable situation by becoming 'bridge fiends' or cross-word puzzle fans, or golfing enthusiasts.

I myself had filled the gaps by dancing. Night after night I had flirted and danced in those past days until I was ready to drop straight to sleep. This was because my sister and I had been 'brought out' whilst I was studying art at the Slade School. I had been mostly too busy and too tired to pay attention to the vague feeling that I was not *really* alive which was nearly always with me. I had felt as if I were the spectator of my own life, the looker-on, as it were, of the half of myself that was trying to live as other people lived, to feel as other people felt. I wondered sometimes if I were normal.

But since the advent of Raphael I seemed to have become really alive, with a deep kind of excitement and exhilaration, and that wonderful thrill which accompanies the passionate search for truth. But would I be able to keep it up all alone? Bereft of Raphael's magical presence, how would I fare?

'My dear student,' came his gentle thrilling voice from behind me, 'I will always be with you *really*. You must try to learn how to master this coat of flesh and overcome its restrictions. Many others have done so, and I have the utmost faith that you too will achieve it!'

'Oh teach me how I shall be able to reach you Raphael,' I cried, urgently swinging round towards him. 'That is all I want to know now!'

'*Why* do you want to know it?' came my teacher's reply in that quiet even tone of which I had learned to beware.

I hesitated and regarded him cautiously.

'I suppose you think I'm going to say that it is purely for selfish reasons – because I don't want to feel I've lost you – because your presence and your teaching are more important to me than anything else in life! Well – it *is*!' I finished desperately. 'And I don't care if you know it!'

'And I suppose you think that I am going to say,' mimicked Raphael with a twinkle in his eye, 'that you must overcome all self-centredness of that kind. You are quite wrong, you know. I am not a kill-joy, and I do not believe in turning oneself into a dutiful machine. I believe it is not of so much importance what one does in life so long as the *motive* is good and so long as one passes on to others the best that one knows. Be sure of these two things, and forget about the rest. Come, let us begin work!'

So saying he took my hand and led me along the path towards my cabin. For this little scene had taken place in my beloved walled garden. Throwing back the two folding

doors, we settled ourselves in a couple of deckchairs. I
sighed with joy. We were facing the moon which hung
silent and mysterious above the dim distant meadow-
land. The world seemed to be holding its breath. The dew
was settling about us, appearing magically upon leaf and
grass-blade and cobweb, each drop reflecting the moon
within its tiny orb.

'It seems a pity to speak,' I whispered.

'You are right,' murmured Raphael. 'Words conceal
more than they reveal. Nevertheless we must make the
best of them! You have a long trail ahead of you, my
friend, and much to go through. I want you always to
bear in mind what it is all for. It is all to give you the
opportunity of interpreting the knowledge you have gained through me, as it applies to daily living. Try and find
out the purpose of all events, of all difficulties and of all
developments. Continue by yourself to discover the secret
of salvation. Realize that through meditation – that is to
say through one-pointed concentration of the mind, you
can discover all you wish to know!'

'But *how?*' I queried.

'The mind is a powerful electrical instrument, very like
a wireless set. That is to say, you can tune in to any
expression of life that you wish, so that you virtually share
that life and all its secrets. Whatever you wish to reach
with your mind you can – even heaven! That is why we
are told that heaven is within us. But remember that what
you *receive* is not your own mental action – any more than
what your radio receives is your radio! Radio and mind
are only instruments, repeaters. But through meditation
you can train your *higher* mind (which few people use as
yet) to achieve creative thought, and tune in to "heaven".'

'Yes, but what *is* heaven?'

'If I were to tell you that it is the mind of God – or
rather, a reflection of it – would that convey anything to
you? And that your mind, having been created by that
greater mind, is also a part of it? Only a microscopic frac-

tion of our full minds is functioning in most of us. What you have to do is to wake your mind up – learn *really* to think! Then you will do much creative and valuable work.'

'Raphael!' I said, feeling a great sadness, 'is this really the last time you will come to teach me?'

'Yes, it is the last time for many, many moons! But to console you, my dear friend, I will let you choose whatever you wish to see this evening!'

I thought deeply for several minutes. Then I raised my head.

'You remember showing me the vision that the middle-aged man had in his crystal globe? Why did he see that particular scene, Raphael?'

'Because his great interest is in learning and knowledge. A crystal globe merely helps you to focus your mind inwards to its own core, where your greatest interest is harboured. *Concentrating* on that interest causes your electrical mind to tune in, as it were, to all connected with that interest. Your mind acts as a sort of television set and you are able to see that which is nearest to your heart, because of a resonance with it!'

'Well, Raphael, then I would like to see *your* vision, that which is nearest to *your* heart and would appear if you looked into *your* crystal globe!' I demanded, very earnestly. There came a long pause. Then my friend raised his head and looked intently at me as he replied.

'Why should you wish thus to probe my innermost secrets, Verity?'

I dropped my eyes, rather ashamed, but answered doggedly. 'If I know the goal of all your hopes I will be able the better to work for them.' I said.

'You win, Verity! Your motive is most uncomfortably right,' said Raphael with a quizzical smile, 'so I find myself constrained to grant your request! Know, then, that I have the utmost faith in the coming of a Golden Age to mankind before many generations have passed;

and that I try always to envisage the future civilization, in order to be able to help people to prepare for it. As you know, many thousands are already expecting the return of Christ, to give us the teaching necessary for the building of the Aquarian Age. For this "Second Coming" great foresight and re-thinking is necessary. Come, Verity, we will go and look in my crystal globe.'

He held out his hand to me and rose from his chair. I sprang up eagerly beside him, forgetting even to notice whether I had left my body behind. We floated rapidly through the glittering moonlight. In less than a minute, it seemed, we were once more in the Halls of Learning, and passing quietly through the busy crowds. We entered a small sanctum furnished with the familiar large crystal globe. Without a word we both sat down and composed ourselves to gaze into it. I had time to notice Raphael's expression of happy anticipation before the crystal clouded over. This reassured me considerably, as I was feeling a little worried at having had the temerity to demand such a personal revelation from the dignified Raphael! Evidently his dreams and hopes were centred in the possibility of a new and better civilization in generations to come. This corresponded with the aspiration which had also been growing in my own heart, and which possibly was the cause of the link between my teacher and myself.

My thoughts were interrupted by a luminous glow which was beginning to play upon my face from the depths of the crystal globe. I leaned closer and peered within. As my eyes began to take in the scene, it almost seemed as if I passed within the globe and became a part of that scene, I felt Raphael come round close to my side and grasp my arm in eager companionship as we began to share his vision.

At first, I could not quite make out what I saw. We seemed to be bathed in soft sunshine which was illuminating a landscape that passed swiftly before our eyes.

'We are travelling in an airship,' explained Raphael,

'and the country which you see below you is the England of the future!'

The panorama upon which we gazed had a very unusual aspect. Instead of looking like a patchwork quilt of meadows and farmland, with an occasional bit of woodland and a rare patch of forest, a reverse arrangement was lying before us. It was a patchwork made of forests of various kinds, laid out not in squares but in designs which seemed to follow the natural contours of the land. There were no hedged-in fields or properties. Instead, the public highways were bordered with broad carpets of grasses, cereals, salads and herbs, which, it could be observed, all the people garnered as they chose, whilst they tended and planted with enthusiasm and delight. Skirting these garden-roads were rich stretches of fruit bushes and fruit trees which grew out of a carpet of ever-fruiting strawberries and other delectable ground-fruits. These stretches of fruit trees were flanked by the forests, which rose up on all sides with a majestic variety of colour and form.

By this time the airship from which my companion and I were taking our view must have been skimming very low over the treetops. Not only that, but we were apparently gazing through windows with a telescopic property, as we were able to observe the smallest details.

Therefore it soon became clear that there was a preponderance of nut trees in the forests. Tall magnificent walnut trees, Spanish chestnuts and maples were to be seen in great quantities. Mulberries, umbrella pines, medlars, quinces and elderberries neighboured each other in never-ending variety. Bees, butterflies and birds could be seen swarming gaily over all this wealth of harvest. Everywhere happy human beings could be seen tending the trees, pruning and gathering superfluous wood, studying the condition of the soil, planning with each other the care of their joint land.

I began to observe more closely the signs of human habitation everywhere. Certainly there were many buildings, but they seemed to take on the quality of their surroundings. They caught the colours of the sunshine, or water, and of green verdure, so that they looked as if built of dragon-flies' wings.

'The houses are made of a kind of glass,' explained Raphael earnestly, 'through which run currents of warmth drawn from atomic energy. Let us inspect them more closely.'

Our airship now began to circle very slowly over a district where the trees seemed less plentiful. I picked out one building after another until I discovered that they were laid out in a regular design something like a large flower such as a daisy. The centre of the design was occupied by a great building from which smaller ones radiated on all sides.

'We are looking at a small community town,' said Raphael. 'That big central building houses all the community's social needs, its club and entertainments centre, health services, industrial unit, prayer sanctuary, and school. It also provides heating, laundry work and many other services for the township. The people live largely on fruit, nuts, salads, and sprouted cereals. There is no cooking as we know it. All the people are artists at handicraft. They make each others' clothes and furniture on a system of exchange and barter. They manage without money as we now understand it. They are self-governed and contribute to the government of their land and also to world government. This is all accomplished quite easily through television. People can have tea with each other by television, receive education and even manage their business. There is hardly any need for local travelling.'

I was entranced.

'It is like paradise!' I cried, 'but could such a wonderful way of living ever really come to pass?'

'Of course it could – and will!' exclaimed Raphael. 'It would come about fairly soon if we could break the world money-complex! We are all slaves to money at present,

196 FROM THE MUNDANE TO THE MAGNIFICENT

because we are first of all slaves to fear – fear for ourselves and our own security. We forget: "Seek ye first the
Kingdom of Heaven and all else shall be added unto you."
Come, now we will go and see London.' Swiftly the airship turned and rose silently through the air.

'I do not hear any engine on this plane,' I remarked.

'All is done by atomic energy,' was the reply. 'It is
noiseless, fumeless and very economical. It is drawn from
the air itself and stored and released by means of the mani-
pulation of vibrations and colour rays. People can even
manufacture it for themselves.

The country over which we now passed seemed if anything to increase in beauty. There were no factory sites or
stretches of ruined mining country, no ugly towns or ad-
vertisement placards, no railway junctions. There seemed
to be no ploughed fields and no cattle. Animals could
occasionally be seen wandering at large in family groups.

'The railway transport is all underground,' said Raphael reading my thoughts. 'Ploughing and digging is
considered to be an obsolete and barbaric habit, together
with coalmining! There is no large-scale cropping. The
biochemistry of all plants and their action on the soil is
carefully studied. Planting is always mixed, so that one
plant helps another, and no soil deficiencies occur. This
plan also keeps away pests. As for animals, they are no
longer exploited either for food or clothing. They are allowed to fulfil the economy of nature. The people have
learned to accept their responsibility towards all living
things. They consider that so long as man himself was a
beast of prey, this influenced the animals, and that it is
now man's duty to eradicate the predatory instinct in the
animal kingdom. They are accomplishing this through the
practice of kidnapping all young animals after they are
weaned, and bringing them up together, on a fleshless
diet. Thus, young rabbits and stoats, foxes and fowls are
all brought up as a family. They are trained also not to
damage crops. When they are nearly adult they are turned

loose. It is found that as soon as animals cease to prey upon each other, nature reduces the birthrate accordingly. (The same would apply with mankind.) Such work with animals and plants forms the most absorbing and soul-satisfying hobby for old and young. Ah, here is London!'

I looked down. At first I could discern nothing but a garden landscape with occasional big buildings. Finally I realized that I was, in fact, gazing upon huge stretches of garden built upon the flat roofs of a great city. There was no smoke, no chimneys, no noisy traffic. Children were playing on the roof-gardens or tending their salad beds. There seemed to be but little street life and hardly any shops.

'As I told you,' explained Raphael, 'people make beautiful things for each other. All are craftsmen along some line. So shops are hardly necessary. All surplus production in food and goods are exchanged with other countries, for things which cannot be produced here.'

'It seems very much of an outdoor life!' I exclaimed, as I gazed at all the happy people absorbed in their different occupations. 'That's all very well in fine weather, but what about the proverbial English climate?'

'All that tree planting has reverted the climate to what nature originally intended,' continued my companion. 'Correct afforestation regulates the moisture, disperses the winds, and subdues both heat and cold. When this is carried out all over the world, under the supervision of the world government, the world climate is changed for the better. Soil erosion is conquered. so are droughts, deserts, famines, floods and hurricanes. It all seems simple and obvious enough to these people, now that they have accomplished it!'

Raphael looked triumphant and delighted. I stole a sidelong glance at him. Evidently his vision meant everything to him – if indeed it was only a vision. I was very bewildered. We had at last reached a familiar part of

London: the River Thames, whose curves were still wind-
ing as majestically as ever towards the sea, but whose
banks, it seemed, had become the playground of the
people. Here again, no ugliness was to be seen. Club-
houses and gardens ran down to the water's edge. People
were tending their fruit trees around the borders of the
little artificial sandy beaches. Everywhere children were
gambolling, swimming or studying, sunbrowned and
strong. Folk-dancing in the open air was in progress along
the banks.

I pulled at Raphael's sleeve and whispered to him
gently, so as not to disturb our enthralled attention.

'Raphael, all this is very desirable and ideal – but what
could possibly happen to change the world so much?'

My friend evidently liked my question. He drew a long
breath which meant, I had learned, that I was going to
receive a lengthy answer.

'Verity, these two world wars are in reality *one* war, and
their repercussions will linger on for decades. They will
have rooted out the terrible complacency in which humanity dwelt at the beginning of this century. Mankind has
determined, with his famous free-will, to learn his lessons
the hard way, through the stimulation of almost out-
rageous suffering and degradation. But evolution *must* go
on, and its stimulation will eventually stir up humanity
so that all the dregs and repressions will rise to the surface.
Thus people will be shown their present state so clearly
that a great worldwide reaction, revulsion and aspiration
will take place. The power of this spiritual revolution will
reorient the total attitude of humanity to such a pitch that
the whole world atmosphere – or aura – will change. This
change will enable the greatest event in world history to
take place. Have you any idea what that will be, Verity?'

'The *greatest* event – but how awesome, Raphael – what
could it possibly be?' I whispered anxiously.

'Actually, you *do* know. But is it not extraordinary how
asleep people still are to the most vital things in life. This

is supposed to be a Christian country. Christ told us that He would come again. The Jews believe in the coming of the Messiah; in the East they await the Matreya. The ancient Egyptians had it all mapped out in their amazing Astrology. They spoke of the Ever-Coming One, who appeared in each great Sign of the Zodiac, to give humanity its next lesson in evolution. Yet, with all our history and our research, we remain blind and asleep to the fact that this is indeed now the "end of the Age" of which Christ spoke, and that therefore his Second Coming is closely upon us – the pulse of destiny is racing – the old and obsolete civilizations will all be broken apart. Humanity will be scattered in all directions. From the débris and the ashes the phoenix of the New Age will arise. A generation of *new* and unconditioned peoples will come to birth to build a new age. And you, Verity, will be working with them.'

Raphael's eyes seemed to be on fire. He took my hand.

'Come!' he said, 'and see the crowning of my vision.'

By now we had left the airship. We entered what appeared to be a large and beautiful college. People were streaming silently into it from all directions. We passed into a great hall at one end of which was an enormous television screen. The people assembled in utter silence, waiting. Raphael gripped my arm. A golden light gradually built up on the screen. It blazed with ever greater intensity until a figure suddenly appeared in its midst. I could hardly bear to look at Him. But He soon began to speak. His words were very few and very slow. They seemed to instil meaning and realization other than physically. I felt a great invisible intercommunication at work in the great hall.

Presently the figure faded out. The people remained silent and immobile, absorbing what had been given to them.

'What you have seen will be a world event, taking place regularly everywhere. It will be the greatest thing in people's lives. In each country initiates will hold regular meditation meetings to amplify and study the new teaching.'

'Of what will the teachings consist, Raphael?'

'They will give understanding of the human being's real function on this planet, of his techniques in helping with the evolution of all the kingdoms in nature; with international relationships and the new world economics; of the pattern of living which will eventually produce a world organism – rather than a world government. This will also result in a *world* religion, in which each faith will find its rightful place.'

I sighed. 'It would be so wonderful, Raphael! But when will it all happen?'

'We will have to go through all the trials inherent in wrong living, such as war, disease, ignorance – until our ultimate revolt arrives, and we realize that we must make a stand for integrity at all costs. This reaction has already begun amongst hundreds of humanitarians – the sort of people who are now writing to you, Verity, from all over the world. During the last quarter of every century inspired pioneers emerge who sow the seeds of progress for the next hundred years. Watch for them, Verity!'

'And what can I do to help?'

'Keep close to all I have shown you, and quietly make it known through writing, speaking and teaching – but only to those who *seek*.'

'Raphael, I cannot bear the thought of parting – .'

Raphael seemed to brace himself together. The atmosphere between us was very tense.

'Perhaps it is hard for me, too,' he replied slowly. 'But we each have to fight our own way out of the chrysalis of the past. No-one can do it for us. Remember that you are an embryonic potential deity, as we all are, and that such a one must develop integrity, will and creativeness. Bear in mind that such is your goal. You will be given every possible test, trial and experience in the polishing process which the soul exerts upon the personality in order to make possible the "Kingdom of Heaven upon Earth".'

'But what does that actually mean, I wonder?'

'It means the spiritual kingdom entering fully into the *conscious* physical world, so that there is no longer any division – any veil between – but this is a state which you are not yet able even to imagine!'

I gazed at Raphael, striving to share the picture which he held before me, awed at the future which he depicted.

'Please, Raphael, what must I especially try to do?' I pleaded, overwhelmed by the extraordinary potential ahead of us all.

My friend considered in his careful way before speaking.

'The most necessary development will be our relationship with all the kingdoms of nature – and I *mean* relationship. You and others will learn how actually to communicate with and be aware of all non-physical beings, from the high world of Devas to the involutionary world of nature spirits. Prepare yourself for this, and by the time I come to you again you will be ready for wonderful developments.'

'*How* do I prepare?'

'By learning not to exploit any of the kingdoms, but to understand how to cooperate with their evolution, and by helping to make restitution for the harm done so far to our planet.'

During this time I had hardly noticed our return to my little cabin: I was listening so earnestly to Raphael.

'Always keep hold, Verity, of the main vision I have given you,' he continued gravely. 'Every time you suffer and fall by the wayside, pick yourself up, recollect who and what you really are, and go on with your destined work with renewed vigour and vision. Remember always that you are on the way to the Second Birth – that escape out of the womb of ignorance and materialism into the freedom of godhood on Earth!'

Raphael had risen to his full height as he uttered these

last thrilling words. He stood before me looking more fine and more gracious than ever.

My heart stood still. I suddenly realized that the moment of parting had come.

'Yes, you are right,' he agreed quietly, 'but realize, my dear disciple, that parting between us does not and never can exist. When you have learned, through meditation to tune in to me, as it were, you will be at one, not only with me, but with *my* teacher also. Now there is something for you to think about! And now I am going to make our parting as easy for you as possible. So watch!'

I could not answer him. My throat was too constricted, and tears were burning behind my eyes. I could only gaze longingly at my dear, dear friend. And as I gazed I began, gradually, to see his aura. At first the lovely blue phosphorescent tinge began to outline his tall figure and to play all over it. Then soft gleaming rays of many colours began to pour out in glistening streams until they formed a glorious oval bubble enveloping him. At his head and his heart were two golden lights. These grew stronger and brighter until they fused together and blinded me to all else. I felt myself to be bathed in this beautiful golden light – to be nourished and strengthened by it. The feeling was so wonderful that I had to relinquish both myself and my sorrow to it.

I became at peace, such a peace as I had never known. I felt that I actually *was* the golden light and that there was nothing any more to be done!

How wonderful it was, quite beyond description.

Gradually, I realized that the golden blaze was lessening, was quietly fading – in fact it seemed now to be only within myself, like a gentle bloom.

I roused myself and looked, looked at the place where Raphael had stood.

But I was quite alone.

Select Bibliography

Bailey, Alice, *A Treatise on Cosmic Fire* (Lucis Trust, London 1950).

Bailey, Alice, *Initiation Human and Solar* (Lucis Press 1976).

Heindel, Max, *The Rosicrucian Cosmo-Conception* (US Rosicrucian Fellowship Press 1967).

Hittleman, Richard, *Be Young with Yoga* (Thomas & Co., Preston, USA).

Reid, Vera, *Towards Aquarius* (The Aquarian Press, London 1971).

Stevens, Henry Bailey, *The Recovery of Culture* (Daniel & Co., England 1971).

Watts, Alan, *The Wisdom of Insecurity* (Rider & Co., London 1975).

Wilson, Frank Avary, *Food Fit for Humans* (C. W. Daniel, UK, 1975).